LOVE *and* MERCY

The Story of Salvation

About Sophia Institute for Teachers

Sophia Institute for Teachers was founded by Catholic educators who wanted something different – inspiring professional development programs and classroom-ready materials that more effectively engage students.

With the goal of nurturing the spiritual, moral, and cultural life of souls, and an abiding respect for the role and work of teachers, we strive to provide materials and programs that are at once enlightening to the mind and ennobling to the heart; faithful and complete, as well as useful and practical.

Printed in the United States of America
Design by Perceptions Design Studio

Love and Mercy: The Story of Salvation
ISBN: 978-1-622823-192

Contents

Acknowledgments

AUTHORS

Jose Gonzalez

Mike Gutzwiller

Steve Jonathan Rummelsburg

Mike Verlander

CONTRIBUTING WRITER

Elisabeth Rochon

EDITOR

Veronica Burchard

DESIGN

Carolyn McKinney
Perceptions Studio, Amherst, NH

ACADEMIC ADVISOR

Daniel Garland, Jr.
Christendom College

FIELD-TESTING TEACHERS

Jacqueline Brown
Sacred Heart School
Hampton, NH

Stephanie Fallavollita
St. Thomas Aquinas School
Derry, NH

David Graver
Bishop Carroll High School
Wichita, KS

Abby Johnsen
Bishop Carroll High School
Wichita, KS

Stacey LaValley Lambert
Catechist
Diocese of Manchester, NH

Aaron Swenson
St. Timothy School
Los Angeles, CA

How to Use This Guide

No textbook or teacher's guide can replace your own witness. Each and every day, offer students your own personal examples and stories. Sharing and modeling your faith will help them effectively encounter the Truth who is Jesus Christ.

Each lesson in this Teacher's Guide is designed as a supplement. Lessons are also designed to be self-contained, so that you may just as easily present a single lesson or all of them. If you are able to teach them all, we recommend presenting them in the order they appear in the book.

Each lesson includes:

- Lesson overview, grade level, and learning goals
- Biblical touchstones
- Connections to the *Catechism* and, where applicable, to the USCCB Curriculum
- Framework
- Sacred art and discussion questions
- Background reading
- Warm-up
- Activities and handouts
- Wrap-Up
- Extension options, including bulletin board ideas, where applicable
- Answer Key

Tips

- Use the sacred art with ALL grade levels.
- Use the Biblical Touchstones for scriptural memorization.
- Let yourself be inspired by lessons even if they are not recommended for the grade you teach.
- You know best what your students already know, so keep that in mind when approaching warm-up exercises, which are meant to recall prior knowledge and/or create a mindset for the lesson.
- Grade level recommendations are merely suggestions. You know your students best.

Occasionally, references are made to additional resources including:

Sophia SketchPad Videos

- Found at **SophiaSketchPad.org**
- Catechetical videos developed for use in Catholic classrooms
- Viewing guides and other supplements

Catholic Curriculum Exchange

- Found at **SophiaInstituteforTeachers.org/Curriculum**
- Teacher-written resources for all subjects and grade-levels
- Digital images of art included in this guide

Laminated art sets

- Available for purchase at **SophiaInstituteforTeachers.org/Shop**

A note on scriptural selections

The translation of the Bible used in this teacher's guide is the New American Bible, Revised Edition (NABRE). For the sake of readability on certain student handouts, we have removed biblical line breaks, line numbers, footnotes, and other references. Whenever possible, we encourage you to have students use their own copies of the Holy Bible to do readings.

Sacred Art and Catechesis
How to Use the Works of Art in This Guide

This Teacher's Guide uses sacred art as a means of teaching young people about the Catholic Faith. Beauty disposes us to the Divine, and sacred art helps lead students to love what is good, beautiful, and true. Art can be viewed and appreciated by all students, no matter their grade, reading ability, personal background, or level of sophistication. Feel free to use these works of art with students of all grade levels. Add your own questions if these are too hard. Say them out loud if students cannot read the questions themselves. Have older students compose their own questions. Have fun.

- Before presenting artwork, we recommend you gather relevant Scripture passages and sections of the *Catechism* to contextualize discussion. Numerous references for each artwork can be found here: **SophiaInstituteforTeachers.org/library/art**.
- We recommend projecting a full-screen image of each work of art, and/or handing out color copies for each student or small group of students.
- Allow students to view the art quietly for several minutes – or for as long as you can. Encourage them to appreciate it for its own sake before beginning any analysis.
- Begin your discussion by asking questions that are easy to answer. This may help "prime the pump" for future discussion.
- Be willing to share your own response to the painting. Allow your students to see the painting move you. Sharing the feelings and ideas the artwork evokes in you may encourage your students to be more willing to take risks in the ways they contribute to the discussion.
- Add your own favorite works of art. Don't be limited to paintings. Think about using sculpture, wood carvings, stained glass, and so forth. Your enthusiasm for works of art will be contagious.

INTRODUCTION

The Christian Faith: A Love Story

by Mike Gutzwiller, Director of Curriculum Development, Sophia Institute for Teachers

At the heart of the Christian life we find love. St. John the Evangelist tells us that God is love and that whoever is without love does not know God because He is love. This profound statement about God unlocks the entire mystery of our faith. Why would an all-powerful, all-knowing, infinite and unchanging God create us weak, sinful, and limited human beings? And further, why would this same transcendent God become one of His creations and die for us the most brutal of deaths? The only satisfying answer to these existential questions is because God is love. In fact, this is the only answer that makes sense at all.

Love is not a verb for God. It is an adjective. It does not so much describe what He does but who He is. God is not the kind of love that gives warm fuzzy feelings in the pit of your stomach. As the song says, love is more than a feeling. God is true love, the kind of love that is self-giving and self-sacrificing, the kind of love a man and woman share in the bonds of marriage whereby they give their entire selves, body and soul, as a free gift to the other. And in the normal course of things, by the grace of God, the love of the husband and wife is fruitful and produces children. The kind of love that God is does not equate with the kind of love our culture preaches. In fact, quite the opposite. True love does not ask "What's in it for me?" but rather, is poured out completely upon the other. True love is unselfish, pure gift, and fruitful. In this understanding of love do we find the answer to the first of the previous existential questions: Why did God create? Because He is love, and love by its very nature, is freely given and is fruitful.

The second of the existential questions above shares the same answer as the first: God is love. God's love is inseparable from His mercy. They are two sides of the same coin. Ask any couple that has been married for many years the secret of their longevity, and almost without exception they will say forgiveness. No marriage will stand the test of time without mercy. Ask any parent the essential quality to successful parenting and again, almost without exception they will say forgiveness, mercy. What parent does not forgive their child his or her transgressions? Perhaps more than any other characterization, love is merciful.

The Catechism of the Catholic Church (no. 734) tells us, "Because we are dead or at least wounded through sin, the first effect of the gift of love is the forgiveness of our sins," and St. John the Evangelist tells us in His Gospel that "God so loved the world that he gave his only Son, so that everyone who believes in him might not perish but might have eternal life. For God did not send his Son into the world to condemn the world, but that the world might be saved through him" (John 3:16-17). Jesus Christ, after revealing the Father's love for us

To love as Christ loves is to imitate Him by embracing His mercy and offering it to one another in sacrifice. This is our calling, our universal vocation of holiness.

The Seven Works of Mercy, by Frans Francken II

through His words and deeds, died on the Cross for us, pouring out God's mercy upon us, for the forgiveness of our sins. St. Paul tells us that the penalty for sin is death, a debt we all owe. By our sins we have grievously offended God. But, like a faithful spouse or a loving parent, God never ceases to offer His love and mercy.

The story of the Christian Faith is a love story, and the protagonists are God and His people. Throughout human history God has pursued us. He has revealed Himself to us and made His love known to us. The *Catechism of the Catholic Church* (no. 218) illuminates this mystery: "In the course of its history, Israel was able to discover that God had only one reason to reveal Himself to them, a single motive for choosing them from among all peoples as His special possession: His sheer gratuitous love. And thanks to the prophets Israel understood that it was again out of love that God never stopped saving them and pardoning their unfaithfulness and sins." Like any epic love story, the story of our Faith is filled with discovery, generosity, tenderness, intimacy, drama, pain, guilt, mercy, and forgiveness. But unlike any other human story of love, God, the pursuer, is unfailingly faithful to His beloved, His Chosen People, us, despite His beloved's persistent unfaithfulness.

We encounter this love story first and foremost in Scripture. The Bible is the written record of the story of our salvation. We call this salvation history, whereby God made Himself known in specific ways, to prepare us, His people, for the gift of salvation. Salvation history is the story of God's saving actions in human history. God entered into a series of covenants with mankind by which He gradually and in stages, in words and deeds, revealed more of Himself and drew us deeper into relationship with Him. Each new covenant contained a sign, taken from human experience, to represent the depth of God's love present at the heart of each covenant. Marriage between a man and woman, the Sabbath, the rainbow, circumcision, the Law, Passover, and the Temple all took on greater meaning in their communication of God's love and mercy.

Finally, at the appointed time, God Himself entered into human history by sending His only beloved Son, the Second Person of the Blessed Trinity, to become human, like us in all things but sin. Jesus fully revealed the Father and communicated His grace to us in and through His life and teaching. He performed miracles as signs of God's love and mercy and to announce the coming of the Kingdom of God. And then he offered Himself as a sacrifice for the sins of many. By His Cross and Resurrection we are freed from sin and made holy. Our salvation has been won!

Jesus tells us to love one another, saying "This is my commandment: love one another as I love you" (John 15:12). Far from the warm fuzzy feelings of the modern notion of love, Jesus tells us to love as He loved. The question is: How did Jesus love us? St. John the Evangelist explains, "In this is love: not that we have loved God, but that he loved us and sent his Son as expiation for our sins" (1 John 4:10). Further, Jesus says, "No one has greater love than this, to lay down one's life for one's friends" (John 15:13). The greatest expression of love is self-sacrifice, giving oneself as a gift to another. On the night before He died, Jesus gathered with His Apostles for their last meal together. He took bread, said the blessing, broke it, and gave it to them saying, "Take and eat; this is my body" (Matthew 26:26). Similarly, He took the cup of wine, gave thanks, and gave it to them saying, "Drink from it, all of you, for this is my blood of the covenant, which will be shed on behalf of many for the forgiveness of sins" (Matthew 16:27). And, the next day, Jesus sacrificed Himself on the Cross, fulfilling His words by His actions. Christ loved us by giving Himself freely and completely to us in an act of mercy.

To love as Christ loves is to imitate Him by embracing His mercy and offering it to one another in sacrifice. This is our calling, our universal vocation of holiness. In response to Christ's command to be perfect as the Father is perfect, the council fathers of Vatican II wrote in *Lumen Gentium*, "In order to reach this perfection, the faithful should use the strength dealt out to them by Christ's gift, so that … doing the will of the Father in everything, they may wholeheartedly devote themselves to the glory of God and to the service of their neighbor." Because God loved us first and poured out His mercy upon us, we are able to serve one another, in love and mercy, encompassed in the petition of the Lord's Prayer: "forgive us our trespasses, as we forgive those who trespass against us." By the grace of God, may we be strengthened to know His love, accept His mercy, and humbly serve our brothers and sisters in the spirit of that very same love and mercy of God.

God's Mercy and His Covenants 

LESSON OVERVIEW

Learning Goals

- Mercy is love that continues even when it is rejected.
- God's mercy is infinite.
- Throughout salvation history, God has sought a relationship with mankind through establishing covenants with us.
- Covenants establish familial bonds and relationships.
- Covenants with man are clear signs of God's mercy toward us.

Connection to the Catechism

- CCC 54-73
- CCC 1846-1848

Essential Questions

- What is mercy?
- What is a covenant?
- What is the difference between a covenant and a contract?
- What are the major covenants God has made with man throughout human history?
- How are these covenants signs of God's mercy?

BIBLICAL TOUCHSTONES

God said to Noah and to his sons with him: See, I am now establishing my covenant with you and your descendants after you and with every living creature that was with you: the birds, the tame animals, and all the wild animals that were with you—all that came out of the ark. I will establish my covenant with you, that never again shall all creatures be destroyed by the waters of a flood; there shall not be another flood to devastate the earth.

GENESIS 9:8-11

But when they continued asking him, he straightened up and said to them, "Let the one among you who is without sin be the first to throw a stone at her." Again he bent down and wrote on the ground. And in response, they went away one by one, beginning with the elders. So he was left alone with the woman before him. Then Jesus straightened up and said to her, "Woman, where are they? Has no one condemned you?" She replied, "No one, sir." Then Jesus said, "Neither do I condemn you. Go, [and] from now on do not sin any more."

JOHN 8:7-11

Christ and the Woman Taken in Adultery

BY VASILY POLENOV (1888)

Oil on Canvas, 1888.

DIGITAL IMAGES AVAILABLE AT **WWW.SOPHIAINSTITUTEFORTEACHERS.ORG**

Sacred Art and Mercy
Christ and the Woman Taken in Adultery

Christ and the Woman Taken in Adultery*, Vasily Polenov, 1888*

Directions: Take some time to quietly view and reflect on the art. Let yourself be inspired in any way that happens naturally. Then think about the questions below, and discuss them with your classmates.

Conversation Questions

1. What is the first word or phrase that comes to your mind when you first look at this painting?
2. What event is depicted in this painting?
3. How does the action in the scene make you feel?
4. The focal point of a painting is the spot where your eye comes to rest. What would you say is the focal point of this painting? Does it have more than one?
5. Who are the main figures or groups of figures in this painting?
6. How would you describe the group of figures on the right? Look at the man in white who is pointing. What does he appear to be demanding?
7. Look at the girl on the bottom left of the painting, with her hand under her chin. If you were to draw a thought bubble over her head, what would it say?
8. If you had to put the people in this painting into three categories, what would those categories be, and who would be in each category?
9. Would you be able to make some sense of what is happening in this painting even if you had not read the Gospel story?
10. How does this painting help show us what mercy is?
11. How do the figures on the right side of this painting understand justice?
12. How is God's mercy revealed in this painting?
13. Are justice and mercy in opposition to each other? If so, how can they be reconciled?
14. If you witnessed this scene in real life, would you be like the figures on the right, the girls on the left, or someone else?
15. Reread the story in John 8:2-11. How does this image help you understand this Gospel passage and the mercy of God?

● ES ▲ MS ■ HS

Lesson Plan

Materials

- Sacred Art and Mercy: Christ and the Woman Taken in Adultery
- Handout A: Scriptural Foundations
- Handout B: Consequences and Relationships
- Handout C: Contracts vs. Covenants
- Teacher Resource: God's Covenants and Mercy Cards
- Handout D: God's Covenants and Mercy

Background/Homework

Have students read **Handout A: Scriptural Foundations** and answer the comprehension and critical thinking questions that follow.

Warm-Up I

A. Display an image of *Christ and the Woman Taken in Adultery* by Vasily Polenov. This image is on **Sacred Art and Mercy: Christ and the Woman Taken in Adultery**. Give students as much time as possible to view the painting in silence. Allow them to come up to the screen to examine details.

B. Put students in pairs or trios and give each group a laminated color copy of **Sacred Art and Mercy: Christ and the Woman Taken in Adultery**. Have students discuss the questions in groups and then share responses as a large group

Warm-Up II

A. Have students complete **Handout B: Consequences and Relationships**.

B. After students have completed the handout, ask the following questions:

- Based on the handout, what would you say is the difference between a contract and a covenant?
- How would you begin to define what a covenant is?

Activity

A. Begin this section by going over key points with the students, using the PowerPoint available on the Catholic Curriculum Exchange at **www.SophiaInstituteforTeachers.org/Curriculum**. You may wish to use **Handout C: Contracts vs. Covenants** with younger learners.

B. Have students work on and complete **Handout D: The Covenants and God's Mercy**.

C. After students have had a chance to complete the handout, take time to go over the answers, emphasizing the connection that God's covenants are a sign of His mercy. Even when man breaks these covenants, God continues to show us love and mercy.

Wrap-Up

A. Read the Rite of Marriage, available at **CatholicLiturgy.com**.

B. After students have completed the reading, pose this question: "How does the covenant of marriage naturally rely on mercy in order to be lived out successfully?"

C. Conclude by saying a Divine Mercy Chaplet as a class.

Extension Option

Explore how forgiveness and mercy work together to strengthen not only God's relationship with us, but also our relationships with others. Using the scenarios in **Handout B** as inspiration, have students work in groups of 3-4 to write original short skits demonstrating how we can learn from God to forgive all offenses, bear wrongs patiently, and practice other Works of Mercy.

HANDOUT A

Scriptural Foundations

Directions: Read the selections and then answer the questions that follow.

John 8:2-11

But early in the morning he arrived again in the temple area, and all the people started coming to him, and he sat down and taught them. Then the scribes and the Pharisees brought a woman who had been caught in adultery and made her stand in the middle. They said to him, "Teacher, this woman was caught in the very act of committing adultery. Now in the law, Moses commanded us to stone such women. So what do you say?" They said this to test him, so that they could have some charge to bring against him. Jesus bent down and began to write on the ground with his finger. But when they continued asking him, he straightened up and said to them, "Let the one among you who is without sin be the first to throw a stone at her." Again he bent down and wrote on the ground. And in response, they went away one by one, beginning with the elders. So he was left alone with the woman before him. Then Jesus straightened up and said to her, "Woman, where are they? Has no one condemned you?" She replied, "No one, sir." Then Jesus said, "Neither do I condemn you. Go, [and] from now on do not sin any more."

Genesis 1:26-27

Then God said: Let us make man in our image, after our likeness. Let them have dominion over the fish of the sea, the birds of the air, the tame animals, all the wild animals, and all the creatures that crawl on the earth. God created man in his image; in the divine image he created them; male and female he created them

Genesis 2:7

Then the LORD God formed the man out of the dust of the ground and blew into his nostrils the breath of life, and the man became a living being.

Cf. Genesis 3:15

I will put enmity between you and the woman, and between your offspring and hers; he will strike at your head, while you strike at his heel.

Genesis 9:8-17

God said to Noah and to his sons with him: See, I am now establishing my covenant with you and your descendants after you and with every living creature that was with you: the birds, the tame animals, and all the wild animals that were with you–all that came out of the ark. I will establish my covenant with you, that never again shall all creatures be destroyed by the waters of a flood; there shall not be another flood to devastate the earth. God said: This is the sign of the covenant that I am making between me and you and every living creature with you for all ages to come: I set my bow in the clouds to serve as a sign of the covenant between me and the earth. When I bring clouds over the earth, and the bow appears in the clouds, I will remember my covenant between me and you and every living creature—every mortal being—so that the waters will never again become a flood to destroy every mortal being. When the bow appears in the clouds, I will see it and remember the everlasting covenant between God and every living creature—every mortal being that is on earth. God told Noah: This is the sign of the covenant I have established between me and every mortal being that is on earth.

Genesis 12:1-3

The LORD said to Abram: Go forth from your land, your relatives, and from your father's house to a land that I will show you. I will make of you a great nation, and I will bless you; I will make your name great, so that you will be a blessing. I will bless those who bless you and curse those who curse you. All the families of the earth will find blessing in you.

Genesis 17:1-13

When Abram was ninety-nine years old, the LORD appeared to Abram and said: I am God the Almighty. Walk in my presence and be blameless. Between you and me I will establish my covenant, and I will multiply you exceedingly. Abram fell face down and God said to him: For my part, here is my covenant with you: you are to become the father of a multitude of nations. No longer will you be called Abram; your name will be Abraham, for I am making you the father of a multitude of nations. I will make you exceedingly fertile; I will make nations of you; kings will stem from you. I will maintain my covenant between me and you and your descendants after you throughout the ages as an everlasting covenant, to be your God and the God of your descendants after you. I will give to you and to your descendants after you the land in which you are now residing as aliens, the whole land of Canaan, as a permanent possession; and I will be their God. God said to Abraham: For your part, you and your descendants after you must keep my covenant throughout the ages. This is the covenant between me and you and your descendants after you that you must keep: every male among you shall be circumcised. Circumcise the flesh of your foreskin. That will be the sign of the covenant between me and you. Throughout the ages, every male among you, when he is eight days old, shall be circumcised, including houseborn slaves and those acquired with money from any foreigner who is not of your descendants. Yes, both the houseborn slaves and those acquired with money must be circumcised. Thus my covenant will be in your flesh as an everlasting covenant.

Exodus 19:1-6

In the third month after the Israelites' departure from the land of Egypt, on the first day, they came to the wilderness of Sinai. After they made the journey from Rephidim and entered the wilderness of Sinai, they then pitched camp in the wilderness. While Israel was encamped there in front of the mountain, Moses went up to the mountain of God. Then the LORD called to him from the mountain, saying: This is what you will say to the house of Jacob; tell the Israelites: You have seen how I treated the Egyptians and how I bore you up on eagles' wings and brought you to myself. Now, if you obey me completely and keep my covenant, you will be my treasured possession among all peoples, though all the earth is mine. You will be to me a kingdom of priests, a holy nation. That is what you must tell the Israelites.

2 Samuel 7:1-16

After the king had taken up residence in his house, and the LORD had given him rest from his enemies on every side, the king said to Nathan the prophet, "Here I am living in a house of cedar, but the ark of God dwells in a tent!" Nathan answered the king, "Whatever is in your heart, go and do, for the LORDis with you." But that same night the word of the LORD came to Nathan: Go and tell David my servant, Thus says the LORD: Is it you who would build me a house to dwell in? I have never dwelt in a house from the day I brought Israel up from Egypt to this day, but I have been going about in a tent or a tabernacle. As long as I have wandered about among the Israelites, did I ever say a word to any of the judges whom I commanded to shepherd my people Israel: Why have you not built me a house of cedar? Now then, speak thus to my servant David, Thus says the LORD of hosts: I took you from the pasture, from following the flock, to become ruler over my people Israel. I was with you wherever you went, and I cut down all your enemies before you. And I will make your name like that of the greatest on earth. I will assign a place for my people Israel and I will plant them in it to dwell there; they will never again be disturbed, nor shall the wicked ever again oppress them, as they did at the beginning, and from the day when I appointed judges over my people Israel. I will give you rest from all your enemies. Moreover, the LORD also declares to you that the LORD will make a house for you: when your days have been completed and you rest with your ancestors, I will raise up your offspring after you, sprung from your loins, and I will establish his kingdom. He it is who shall build a house for my name, and I will establish his royal throne forever. I will be a father to him, and he shall be a son to me. If he does wrong, I will reprove him with a human rod and with human punishments; but I will not withdraw my favor from him as I withdrew it from Saul who was before you. Your house and your kingdom are firm forever before me; your throne shall be firmly established forever.

Luke 1:26-38

In the sixth month, the angel Gabriel was sent from God to a town of Galilee called Nazareth, to a virgin betrothed to a man named Joseph, of the house of David, and the virgin's name was Mary. And coming to her, he said, "Hail, favored one! The Lord is with you." But she was greatly troubled at what was said and pondered what sort of greeting this might be. Then the angel said to her, "Do not be afraid, Mary, for you have found favor with God. Behold, you will conceive in your womb and bear a son, and you shall name him Jesus. He will be great and will be called Son of the Most High, and the Lord God will give him the throne of David his father, and he will rule over the house of Jacob forever, and of his kingdom there will be no end." But Mary said to the angel, "How can this be, since I have no relations with a man?" And the angel said to her in reply, "The holy Spirit will come upon you, and the power of the Most High will overshadow you. Therefore the child to be born will be called holy, the Son of God. And behold, Elizabeth, your relative, has also conceived a son in her old age, and this is the sixth month for her who was called barren; for nothing will be impossible for God." Mary said, "Behold, I am the handmaid of the Lord. May it be done to me according to your word." Then the angel departed from her.

Luke 22:14-20

When the hour came, he took his place at table with the apostles. He said to them, "I have eagerly desired to eat this Passover with you before I suffer, for, I tell you, I shall not eat it [again] until there is fulfillment in the kingdom of God." Then he took a cup, gave thanks, and said, "Take this and share it among yourselves; for I tell you [that] from this time on I shall not drink of the fruit of the vine until the kingdom of God comes." Then he took the bread, said the blessing, broke it, and gave it to them, saying, "This is my body, which will be given for you; do this in memory of me." And likewise the cup after they had eaten, saying, "This cup is the new covenant in my blood, which will be shed for you.

Critical Thinking Questions

1. What does the story from the Gospel of John reveal to us about who Jesus is and what He desires for us?
2. What do all of these passages have in common?
3. The passage from the Gospel of John may seem to be out of place here. How does it still fit in and connect with the other passages?
4. What does each of these passages ultimately reveal about God and His plan for us?
5. What truths about who we are as human beings can you come up with based on these passages from Scripture?

HANDOUT B

Consequences and Relationships

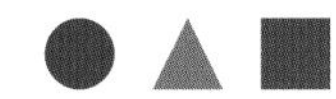

Directions: Briefly describe what you think the consequence might be for each of the following scenarios.

1. You hire someone to put in new windows and siding on your house. He does a very poor job and causes damage to your home.

____

____

____

2. You accept a new job that will pay you a salary. You fail to show up for work regularly, and when you do show up, you are late and you fail to meet deadlines.

____

____

____

3. A student brings a gun to school and threatens other students.

____

____

____

4. Your parents give you a curfew. You get home two hours late.

____

____

____

5. A wife goes out to run errands for the day and asks her husband to do some things around the house. He agrees. She posts the list of things she needs done on the refrigerator. He spends all day watching sports and relaxing on the couch and doesn't do any of the things on his wife's list.

____

____

____

6. After reflecting on the above scenarios answer the following questions:

____

____

____

7. What are the differences between the first three scenarios and the last two?

____

____

____

8. How do the consequences between the first set and the second set of scenarios differ?

____

____

____

9. What set of scenarios is our relationship with God more like? Explain.

____

____

____

HANDOUT C

Contracts vs. Covenants

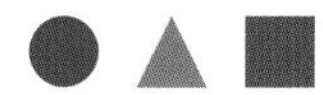

Directions: Complete the chart using the information below, information from your teacher, and your own knowledge.

The *Catechism* defines mercy as "the loving kindness, compassion, or forbearance shown to one who offends." Mercy can also be defined as love that keeps on loving even when it is rejected. God has revealed His mercy to us through covenants in salvation history. Covenant comes from the Latin word *convenire*, which means "to come together" or "to agree," and it is the central theme throughout Scripture. A covenant is a formal and solemn pact or agreement permanently binding two or more parties to responsibilities toward each other.

Contracts	**Covenants**
Exchange of ________________.	Exchange of ________________.
Sets up obligations, but they are not ________________ obligations.	There are personal responsibilities that flow from a covenant. These responsibilities are based on ________________.
The basis of contractual obligations is ________________.	Covenants are based on ________________.
It is a conditional/unconditional relationship. (*circle one*)	It is a conditional/unconditional relationship. (circle one)
It is a 50/50 relationship.	It is a ________________ relationship.

God's Covenants and Mercy Cards

Note: Make as many copies of the grid below as you have students. Cut out into cards, and shuffle them. Give one set of cards to each student in order to complete **Handout B**.

Adam	God called him to share in His blessings in the marriage covenant.	**Sabbath**	**One Holy Couple**
Noah	God pledged to keep him and his family safe from the flood and then swore never to wipe out the human family in that way again.	**Rainbow**	**One Holy Family**
Abraham	God promised that he would be the father of a host of nations, with descendants as numerous as the stars.	**Circumcision**	**One Holy Tribe**

Moses	The Lord used him to lead Israel out of slavery in Egypt and pledged to the people through him that they would occupy the promised land of Canaan.	**Passover/The Law**	**One Holy Nation**
David	God made a covenant with him to build a worldwide Kingdom by establishing an everlasting throne with His son.	**Throne/ Temple**	**One Holy Kingdom**
Jesus	This covenant fulfills all other covenants and pledges eternal life to all who believe.	**The Eucharist**	**One Holy Catholic Church**

HANDOUT D

God's Covenants and Mercy

Directions: Every covenant has a promise, a mediator, and a sign. Each covenant also signifies a progression or growth in God's family. Fill in the following chart by placing the squares you receive in the appropriate space. Once you have completed the chart, answer the questions that follow.

Covenant Mediator	Covenant Promise	Covenant Sign	Covenant Progression
Adam			
Noah			
Abraham			

Covenant Mediator	Covenant Promise	Covenant Sign	Covenant Progression
Moses			
David			
Jesus			

1. What does each of these covenants communicate about God's love for us?

2. How is God's mercy revealed and manifested to us more deeply with each covenant?

Answer Key

Handout A: Scriptural Foundations

1. Jesus is merciful and desires us to be in relationship with Him. Accept additional reasoned answers.
2. They are all about God establishing some kind of relationship or commitment with someone.
3. It is about God restoring a relationship that has been broken by man. It is a story about God's love for humanity just like the others.
4. God desires us to be in relationship with Him. He desires that we live our lives in union with Him. If we follow His laws, we will be happy and fulfilled.
5. We are made for love and to be loved. We often search for this need and find ways to fill it in other ways. We can be truly happy only by living in God's love.

Handout B: Consequences and Relationships

1. You may refuse to pay the company. You may take them to court. You will almost certainly find a new company with which to do business. Accept additional reasoned answers.
2. You will get fired. Accept additional reasoned answers.
3. The student will be expelled (and likely arrested). Students may become distracted by the fact that this scenario does not include an actual contact, as is the case in numbers 1 and 2. Remind them that only rarely do our relationships with others involve an actual paper contract. In this example, there are "unwritten" understandings and expectations among classmates, teachers, administrators, etc. There are also written ones such as school rules, student handbooks, and our system of laws that punish violence. These go beyond a literal contract, but do not rise to the level of the permanently binding covenants in the next two scenarios. Accept additional reasoned answers.
4. Your parents will punish you. You will lose their trust. Accept additional reasoned answers.
5. The husband might have to do some extra things around the house to make up for his laziness. He might have to buy his wife some flowers. His wife might avoid speaking to him for a little while to show she is upset and has lost trust in him. She might forgive him because he works hard all week to support them and needs a little downtime, even if he forgot to speak up about that fact before she left. Accept additional reasoned answers.

6. The first three scenarios deal with contractual obligations. The last two deal with relationships and respecting the love and trust of those closest to us.
7. The consequences in the first three scenarios sever the relationships. The contracts become null and void. In the last two they may hurt or damage the relationship but the relationship and mutual obligations do not cease to exist. A parent would not disown his or her child for breaking a rule. If marriage vows are lived seriously and respected, a disagreement would not result in the ending of that relationship.
8. Accept reasoned answers, but students should recognize it is more like the last two scenarios.

Handout C: Contracts vs. Covenants

Contracts	Covenants
Exchange of goods and services.	Exchange of persons
Sets up obligations, but they are not deeply personal obligations.	There are personal responsibilities and mutual obligations that flow from covenants. These responsibilities are based on our personal relationship and commitment to the other person.
These obligations are based merely on human words and promises.	These are based on God's word.
It is a conditional relationship.	These relationships are permanently binding.
It is a 50/50 relationship.	Not a 50/50 relationship; it is a 100/100.

Love and Mercy Revealed: The Covenant with Adam

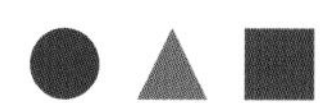

LESSON OVERVIEW

Learning Goals

- God creates out of love.
- Even the story of the Fall reveals God's mercy and love.
- Although man rejected God, God's mercy never faded. He began a plan to draw man back to Himself.

Connection to the Catechism

- CCC 282-301
- CCC 355-421

Essential Questions

- Why did God create us?
- How is God's plan for our redemption present even from the beginning?
- Why do we refer to Jesus as the new Adam and Mary as the new Eve?

BIBLICAL TOUCHSTONES

I will put enmity between you and the woman, and between your offspring and hers; he will strike at your head, while you strike at his heel.

CF. GENESIS 3:15

While he was speaking, a woman from the crowd called out and said to him, "Blessed is the womb that carried you and the breasts at which you nursed." He replied, "Rather, blessed are those who hear the word of God and observe it."

LUKE 11:27-28

Adam and Eve in the Garden of Eden

BY LUCAS CRANACH THE ELDER (1450)

Oil on wood, 11 x 69.5 cm, Musée des Beaux Arts, Lille.

DIGITAL IMAGES AVAILABLE AT **WWW.SOPHIAINSTITUTEFORTEACHERS.ORG**

Sacred Art and Mercy
Adam and Eve in the Garden of Eden

Adam and Eve in the Garden of Eden, *Lucas Cranach,* 1450

Directions: Take some time to quietly view and reflect on the art. Let yourself be inspired in any way that happens naturally. Then think about the questions below, and discuss them with your classmates.

Conversation Questions

1. How would you describe the scene in this painting?
2. Which biblical stories are depicted?
3. Which event is depicted in the center of the painting at the bottom? Why do you think the artist chose this image as the central and largest one?
4. How do you think this artist views God?
5. What insights does the painting give us to help us understand who God is?
6. How is the idea of covenant depicted in this painting?

● ES ▲ MS ■ HS

Lesson Plan

Materials

- Sacred Art and Mercy: Adam and Even in the Garden of Eden
- Handout A: Scriptural Foundations
- Handout B: God's Mercy and the Fall
- Handout C: Readings on the New Adam and the New Eve
- Handout D: The New Adam and the New Eve (versions 1, 2, and 3)

Background/Homework

Have students read **Handout A: Scriptural Foundations** and answer the comprehension and critical thinking questions.

Warm-Up I

A. Display an image of *Adam and Eve in the Garden of Eden* by Lucas Cranach the Elder. This image is on **Sacred Art and Mercy: Adam and Eve in the Garden**. Give students as much time as possible to view the painting in silence. Allow them to come up to the screen to examine details.

B. Put students in pairs or trios and give each group a laminated color copy of **Sacred Art and Mercy: Adam and Eve in the Garden**. Have students discuss the questions in groups and then share responses as a large group.

Warm-Up II

A. Have students close their eyes and listen to the passage from Scripture you are about to read. Ask them to try as hard as they can to listen to it as if they are hearing it for the first time.

B. Read one of the following passages from Genesis:

- Genesis 1:1-2:3
- Genesis 2:4-25

C. After you have read one of the two passages, write the following questions on the board and ask the students to take a few moments to write a short reflection in response to them:

- How does this passage remind us of our origins and the purpose for which we are created?
- How does listening to this passage inform us of our destiny?
- How does listening to this passage help us come to know God more fully?
- How does this passage help us understand and encounter the mercy of God?

D. Go over the answers to the questions on **Handout A**.

Activity

A. Begin by briefly going over the following points with students:

- In Genesis 1 we see the first story of Creation. God is revealed as an all-powerful Creator. This first story is like a camera that zooms out and gives us an overview or bird's-eye view of Creation. It teaches us that God is loving and generous. He did not have to create us, but He chose to share His beauty and majesty with His creation.
- In Genesis 2 God is revealed as a loving Father who desires to have a relationship with us. In the second story of Creation, the camera zooms in and focuses on the creation of man. We learn that:
- Like any good Father, God sets rules and limitations for His children through the instructions and commands He gives Adam.
- Man is made for communion and relationship with others. God creates Eve as a partner for Adam.
- The spouses lived in perfect harmony with God, each other, and creation.

B. Have students reread Genesis 3 and complete **Handout B: God's Mercy and the Fall** with a partner. Note: *With younger students, you could also treat the content on* ***Handout B*** *as a mini lecture, using the answer key as a guide.*

C. Go over and review the answers to **Handout B**.

D. Preview and select excerpts for students to read from **Handout C: Readings on the New Adam and the New Eve**. Note: *the selections vary from simple to more complex. Choose the ones from which you believe your students would benefit.*

E. Have students complete **Handout D: The New Adam and the New Eve Chart**. Use version 1, 2, or 3, depending on student age and sophistication.

Variation: You might want to have students complete **Handouts C** and **D** in pairs, with half the class working on Christ as the New Adam and the other half on Mary as the New Eve. Then have them share their findings with the class.

Wrap-Up

A. Project the image *Mary Consoles Eve* by Sr. Grace Remington, O.C.S.O. The image can be found on the last page of **Handout C or** in the Document Library of the Sophia Institute for Teachers website: **www.SophiaInstituteforTeachers.org**

B. Conclude by having a class discussion using the following questions:

   1. What details catch your eye in this image?
   2. How do you see Genesis 3:15 fulfilled in this image?
   3. Why is it a fitting one to end on today?
   4. A title of the Blessed Virgin Mary is Mary, Mother of Mercy. How do you see that title present in this image?
   5. How does this image show us both the seriousness of sin and God's infinite mercy?

HANDOUT A

Scriptural Foundations 

Directions: Read the selections and then answer the questions that follow.

Genesis 1:26-31

Then God said: Let us make man in our image, after our likeness. Let them have dominion over the fish of the sea, the birds of the air, the tame animals, all the wild animals, and all the creatures that crawl on the earth. God created man in his image; in the image of God he created them; male and female he created them. God blessed them and God said to them: Be fertile and multiply; fill the earth and subdue it. Have dominion over the fish of the sea, the birds of the air, and all the living things that crawl on the earth. God also said: See, I give you every seed-bearing plant on all the earth and every tree that has seed-bearing fruit on it to be your food; and to all the wild animals, all the birds of the air, and all the living creatures that crawl on the earth, I give all the green plants for food. And so it happened. God looked at everything he had made, and found it very good. Evening came, and morning followed—the sixth day.

Genesis 2

Thus the heavens and the earth and all their array were completed. On the seventh day God completed the work he had been doing; he rested on the seventh day from all the work he had undertaken. God blessed the seventh day and made it holy, because on it he rested from all the work he had done in creation.

This is the story of the heavens and the earth at their creation. When the LORD God made the earth and the heavens there was no field shrub on earth and no grass of the field had sprouted, for the LORD God had sent no rain upon the earth and there was no man to till the ground, but a stream was welling up out of the earth and watering all the surface of the ground – then the LORD God formed the man out of the dust of the ground and blew into his nostrils the breath of life, and the man became a living being. The LORD God planted a garden in Eden, in the east, and placed there the man whom he had formed. Out of the ground the LORD God made grow every tree that was delightful to look at and good for food, with the tree of life in the middle of the garden and the tree of the knowledge of good and evil. A river rises in Eden to water the garden; beyond there it divides and becomes four branches. The name of the first is the Pishon; it is the one that winds through the whole land of Havilah, where there is gold. The gold of that land is good; bdellium and lapis lazuli are also there. The name of the second river is the Gihon; it is the one that winds all through the land of Cush. The name of the third river is the Tigris; it is the one that flows east of Asshur. The fourth river is the Euphrates. The LORD

God then took the man and settled him in the garden of Eden, to cultivate and care for it. The LORD God gave the man this order: You are free to eat from any of the trees of the garden except the tree of knowledge of good and evil. From that tree you shall not eat; when you eat from it you shall die. The LORD God said: It is not good for the man to be alone. I will make a helper suited to him. So the LORD God formed out of the ground all the wild animals and all the birds of the air, and he brought them to the man to see what he would call them; whatever the man called each living creature was then its name. The man gave names to all the tame animals, all the birds of the air, and all the wild animals; but none proved to be a helper suited to the man. So the LORD God cast a deep sleep on the man, and while he was asleep, he took out one of his ribs and closed up its place with flesh. The LORD God then built the rib that he had taken from the man into a woman. When he brought her to the man, the man said:

"This one, at last, is bone of my bones and flesh of my flesh;
This one shall be called 'woman,' for out of man this one has been taken."

That is why a man leaves his father and mother and clings to his wife, and the two of them become one body. The man and his wife were both naked, yet they felt no shame.

Genesis 3

Now the snake was the most cunning of all the wild animals that the LORD God had made. He asked the woman, "Did God really say, 'You shall not eat from any of the trees in the garden'?" The woman answered the snake: "We may eat of the fruit of the trees in the garden; it is only about the fruit of the tree in the middle of the garden that God said, 'You shall not eat it or even touch it, or else you will die.' " But the snake said to the woman: "You certainly will not die! God knows well that when you eat of it your eyes will be opened and you will be like gods, who know good and evil." The woman saw that the tree was good for food and pleasing to the eyes, and the tree was desirable for gaining wisdom. So she took some of its fruit and ate it; and she also gave some to her husband, who was with her, and he ate it. Then the eyes of both of them were opened, and they knew that they were naked; so they sewed fig leaves together and made loincloths for themselves. When they heard the sound of the LORD God walking about in the garden at the breezy time of the day, the man and his wife hid themselves from the LORD God among the trees of the garden. The LORD God then called to the man and asked him: Where are you? He answered, "I heard you in the garden; but I was afraid, because I was naked, so I hid." Then God asked: Who told you that you were naked? Have you eaten from the tree of which I had forbidden you to eat? The man replied, "The woman whom you put here with me–she gave me fruit from the tree, so I ate it." The LORD God then asked the woman: What is this you have done? The woman answered, "The snake tricked me, so I ate it." Then the LORD God said to the snake:

Because you have done this, cursed are you among all the animals, tame or wild;
On your belly you shall crawl, and dust you

shall eat all the days of your life. I will put enmity between you and the woman, and between your offspring and hers; He will strike at your head, while you strike at his heel.

To the woman he said:

I will intensify your toil in childbearing; in pain you shall bring forth children. Yet your urge shall be for your husband, and he shall rule over you.

To the man he said:

Because you listened to your wife and ate from the tree about which I commanded you, You shall not eat from it, Cursed is the ground because of you! In toil you shall eat its yield all the days of your life. Thorns and thistles it shall bear for you, and you shall eat the grass of the field. By the sweat of your brow you shall eat bread, Until you return to the ground, from which you were taken; For you are dust, and to dust you shall return.

The man gave his wife the name "Eve," because she was the mother of all the living. The LORD God made for the man and his wife garments of skin, with which he clothed them. Then the LORD God said: See! The man has become like one of us, knowing good and evil! Now, what if he also reaches out his hand to take fruit from the tree of life, and eats of it and lives forever? The LORD God therefore banished him from the garden of Eden, to till the ground from which he had been taken. He expelled the man, stationing the cherubim and the fiery revolving sword east of the garden of Eden, to guard the way to the tree of life.

Comprehension and Critical Thinking Questions

1. What sets man apart from the rest of God's creation?
2. What instructions does God give to Adam in Genesis 2?
3. What rule does God give to Adam in Genesis 2?
4. What does the sacred author mean by saying that Adam and Eve were both naked yet felt no shame?
5. How does Eve fall prey to the serpent?
6. Where was Adam while the serpent was speaking to Eve?
7. Why do you think the sin is traditionally referred to as Adam's sin, even though Eve was the first to eat?
8. What are the consequences for the serpent, Eve, and Adam?
9. How is it possible that God kept loving Adam and Eve, even though He punished them?

HANDOUT B

God's Mercy and the Fall

Directions: Reread Genesis 3 and answer the following questions:

1. The story of Creation and the Fall is often used as an example of justice. How does it also show us God's mercy?

____

____

____

____

2. Where in the text of Genesis 3 can you find clear evidence for God's mercy?

____

____

____

____

3. In Genesis, God tells the serpent, "I will put enmity between you and the woman, and between your offspring and hers; he will strike at your head, while you strike at his heel" (cf. 3:15). This verse is referred to as the *Protoevangelium*, which is Greek for "first proclamation of the Gospel." Why do you think it is called that?

____

____

____

____

4. Knowing what you know about the remainder of the story in Scripture, how can you see that God's infinite mercy truly begins to be revealed in this third chapter of Genesis?

____

____

____

____

5. The following lines are from the *Exsultet*, which is sung during the Easter Vigil:

   "O truly necessary sin of Adam, destroyed completely by the Death of Christ! O happy fault that earned so great, so glorious a Redeemer!"

   What is the "happy fault" referred to here? How does this line give us great insight into the mercy of God?

____

____

____

____

The Annunciation, Bl. Fra Angelico

HANDOUT C

Readings on the New Adam and the New Eve

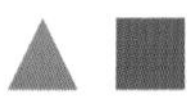

Romans 5:12-18

Therefore, just as through one person sin entered the world, and through sin, death, and thus death came to all, inasmuch as all sinned – for up to the time of the law, sin was in the world, though sin is not accounted when there is no law. But death reigned from Adam to Moses, even over those who did not sin after the pattern of the trespass of Adam, who is the type of the one who was to come. But the gift is not like the transgression. For if by that one person's transgression the many died, how much more did the grace of God and the gracious gift of the one person Jesus Christ overflow for the many. And the gift is not like the result of the one person's sinning. For after one sin there was the judgment that brought condemnation; but the gift, after many transgressions, brought acquittal. For if, by the transgression of one person, death came to reign through that one, how much more will those who receive the abundance of grace and of the gift of justification come to reign in life through the one person Jesus Christ. In conclusion, just as through one transgression condemnation came upon all, so through one righteous act acquittal and life came to all.

Lumen gentium, no. 56

The Father of mercies willed that the Incarnation should be preceded by assent on the part of the predestined mother, so that just as a woman had a share in bringing about death, so also a woman should contribute to life.

Excerpt from *Against Heresies* by St. Irenaeus of Lyons: Mary as the New Eve

The Lord, coming into his own creation in visible form, was sustained by his own creation which he himself sustains in being. His obedience on the tree of the cross reversed the disobedience at the tree in Eden; the good news of the truth announced by an angel to Mary, a virgin subject to a husband, undid the evil lie that seduced Eve, a virgin espoused to a husband.

As Eve was seduced by the word of an angel and so fled from God after disobeying his word, Mary in her turn was given the good news by the word of an angel, and bore God in obedience to his word. As Eve was seduced into disobedience to God, so Mary was persuaded into obedience to God; thus the Virgin Mary became the advocate of the virgin Eve.

Christ gathered all things into one, by gathering them into himself. He declared war against our enemy, crushed him who at the beginning had taken us captive in Adam, and trampled on his head, in accordance with God's words to the serpent in Genesis: I will put enmity between you and the woman, and between your seed and her seed; he shall lie in wait for your head, and you shall lie in wait for his heel.

The one lying in wait for the serpent's head is the one who was born in the likeness of Adam from the woman, the Virgin. This is the seed spoken of by Paul in the letter to the Galatians: The law of works was in force until the seed should come to whom the promise was made.

He shows this even more clearly in the same letter when he says: When the fullness of time had come, God sent his Son, born of a woman. The enemy would not have been defeated fairly if his vanquisher had not been born of a woman, because it was through a woman that he had gained mastery over man in the beginning, and set himself up as man's adversary.

That is why the Lord proclaims himself the Son of Man, the one who renews in himself that first man from whom the race born of woman was formed; as by a man's defeat our race fell into the bondage of death, so by a man's victory we were to rise again to life.

Excerpt from Dec. 3, 2008, General Audience of Pope Benedict XVI, "The apostle's teaching on the relation between Adam and Christ"

Dear Brothers and Sisters,

In today's Catechesis we shall reflect on the relations between Adam and Christ, defined by St. Paul in the well-known passage of the Letter to the Romans (5:12-21) in which he gives the Church the essential outline of the doctrine on original sin. Indeed, Paul had already introduced the comparison between our first progenitor and Christ while addressing faith in the Resurrection in the First Letter to the Corinthians: "For as in Adam all die, so also in Christ shall all be made alive. ...The first man Adam became a living being; the last Adam became a life-giving spirit" (1 Cor. 15:22, 45). With Romans 5:12-21, the comparison between Christ and Adam becomes more articulate and illuminating: Paul traces the history of salvation from Adam to the Law and from the latter to Christ. At the centre of the scene it is not so much Adam, with the consequences of his sin for humanity, who is found as much as it is Jesus Christ and the grace which was poured out on humanity in abundance through him. The repetition of the "all the more" with regard to Christ stresses that the gift received in him far surpasses Adam's sin and its consequent effects on humanity, so that Paul could reach his conclusion: "but where sin increased, grace abounded all the more" (Rom. 5:20). The comparison that Paul draws between Adam and Christ therefore sheds light on the inferiority of the first man compared to the prevalence of the second.

On the other hand, it is precisely in order to highlight the immeasurable gift of grace in Christ that Paul mentions Adam's sin. One could say that if it were not to demonstrate the centrality of grace, he would not have dwelt on the treatment of sin which "came into the world through one man and death through sin" (Rom 5:12). For this reason, if, in the faith of the Church, an awareness of the dogma of original sin developed, it is because it is inseparably linked to another dogma, that of salvation and freedom in Christ. The consequence of this is that we must never treat the sin of Adam and of humanity separately from the salvific context, in other words, without understanding them within the horizon of justification in Christ....

How was it possible, how did it happen? This remains obscure. Evil is not logical. Only God and good are logical, are light. Evil remains mysterious. It is presented as such in great images, as it is in chapter 3 of Genesis, with that scene of the two trees, of the serpent, of sinful man: a great image that makes us guess but cannot explain what is itself illogical. We may guess, not explain; nor may we recount it as one fact beside another, because it is a deeper reality. It remains a mystery of darkness, of night. But a mystery of light is immediately added. Evil comes from a subordinate source. God with his light is stronger. And therefore evil can be overcome. Thus the creature, man, can be healed. The dualist visions, including the monism of evolutionism, cannot say that man is curable; but if evil comes only from a subordinate source, it remains true that man is healable. And the Book of Wisdom says: "he made the nations of the world curable" (1: 14 Vulgate). And finally, the last point: man is not only healable,

Virgin Mary Consoles Eve, Sr. Grace Remington, OCSO

but is healed de facto. God introduced healing. He entered into history in person. He set a source of pure good against the permanent source of evil. The Crucified and Risen Christ, the new Adam, counters the murky river of evil with a river of light. And this river is present in history: we see the Saints, the great Saints but also the humble saints, the simple faithful. We see that the stream of light which flows from Christ is present, is strong.

HANDOUT D

The New Adam and the New Eve

Directions: Fill in the two charts below by using the readings on **Handout D** along with the text of Genesis 3. Write in qualities or events that pertain to Adam and Eve and how they are fulfilled or brought to perfection by Christ and Mary.

Adam	Christ

Eve	Mary

How does understanding Christ as the new Adam and Mary as the new Eve give us greater insight into the mercy of God?

____

____

HANDOUT D

The New Adam and the New Eve

Directions: Fill in the two charts below by using the readings on **Handout D** along with the text of Genesis 3. Write in qualities or events that pertain to each person and how they are fulfilled or brought to perfection by Christ and Mary.

Adam	Christ
Committed the original _______.	Led a _________ life.
Brought _________ through his sin.	Brought _________through sinlessness.
Was disobedient and cursed all.	Was __________ and __________all.
Was conquered by the _________ of knowledge of good and evil and brought _________.	Was nailed to a tree (the Cross) and ___________________ death.

Eve	Mary
Eve, a __________ woman was seduced by a lie.	Mary, a virgin subject to a husband, undid the ________________.
Eve was seduced by the word of __________________ and so ________________ from God after disobeying His word.	Mary in her turn was given the good news by the word of ________________, and ________________ God in obedience to His word.
Eve was seduced into _______________ to God.	Mary was ___________________ into ___________________ to God.

How does understanding Christ as the new Adam and Mary as the new Eve give us greater insight into the mercy of God?

____

____

HANDOUT D

The New Adam and the New Eve

Directions: Read the information comparing Adam and Christ, along with Eve and Mary. Then draw a picture of each one in the space below.

Adam	Christ
› Sinned › Brought death through his sin › Was disobedient › Damaged us all › Was conquered by the tree of knowledge of good and evil	› Sinless › Brought life through His sinlessness › Was obedient › Redeems us all › Was nailed to a tree (the Cross) but conquered death

Eve	Mary
› A married woman › Tricked by a lie › Followed her own judgment rather than God's › Was seduced by the word of a fallen angel (Lucifer) › Fled from God after disobeying His word › Brought sin and death into the world	› A virgin subject to a husband › Undid the evil lie that seduced Eve. › Freely obeyed God's will › Given the good news by the word of an angel › Bore God in obedience to his word. › Brought life into the world

Answer Key

Handout A: Scriptural Foundations

1. We are made in God's image and likeness. We are created with an intellect and free will.
2. "The LORD God then took the man and settled him in the garden of Eden, to cultivate and care for it." In other words, Adam is supposed to protect the garden.
3. "The LORD God gave the man this order: You are free to eat from any of the trees of the garden except the tree of knowledge of good and evil. From that tree you shall not eat; when you eat from it you shall die."
4. That there was no lust in their relationship. They each had a perfect love for the other.
5. There is a serpent in the Garden. Adam is supposed to be protecting the garden.
6. Adam was with Eve. ("She also gave some to her husband, who was with her.")
7. Adam failed to protect his bride. While Eve is to blame for her choice, Adam should have been willing to lay down his life for Eve and protect her from the serpent.
8. Serpent: cursed among animals, "On your belly you shall crawl, and dust you shall eat all the days of your life. I will put enmity between you and the woman, and between your offspring and hers; he will strike at your head, while you strike at his heel." Woman: "I will intensify your toil in childbearing; in pain you shall bring forth children. Yet your urge shall be for your husband, and he shall rule over you." Man: "Cursed is the ground because of you! In toil you shall eat its yield all the days of your life. Thorns and thistles it shall bear for you, and you shall eat the grass of the field. By the sweat of your brow you shall eat bread, Until you return to the ground, from which you were taken; For you are dust, and to dust you shall return."
9. Actions have consequences. Just as any good father allows the consequences of the actions of his children, so God allows consequences to take effect for His children. This does not mean He loves them any less. In fact this signifies His love for His children even more. Accept additional reasoned answers.

Handout B: God's Mercy and the Fall

1. An offense against an infinite God is only justly repaid by instant death. God could have obliterated Adam and Eve; however, He allowed them to live and experience His love, albeit in a more distant way. Punishments also exhibit mercy because consequences can often lead to conversion.
2. God punishes the serpent. This shows He is looking out for His children and is merciful toward them. He punishes and curses that which influenced them to sin. He also

clothes Adam and Eve as they leave the garden. This gift shows He still loves and cares for them and will continue to provide for their needs.

3. God tells the serpent that He will be defeated. He also put "enmity" between the woman and the serpent. Enmity means total opposition. There cannot be true enmity between Eve and the serpent because Eve has just sinned. The only woman to have true enmity with the serpent must be a sinless one. This one is Mary, and her offspring is Christ. God is promising salvation to Adam and Eve immediately after they have sinned.

4. God does not abandon His children after the Fall. He continues to pursue humanity and reveal Himself to them throughout salvation history. God's desire to love and forgive us even though we have rejected Him is made manifest from the moment of man's first sin.

5. The "happy fault" referred to is Adam's sin. Accept reasoned answers. Students may say that we would not have known Christ or Mary without the sin of Adam, and the Exsultet sings of gratitude for God's mercy, which was born out of the rejection caused by Adam and Eve. God's love will always be greater than any evil in this world.

Handout D: The New Adam and the New Eve

Adam	Christ
› Sinned › Brought death through his sin › Was disobedient and cursed all › Was conquered by the tree of knowledge of good and evil and brought death. › Accept additional reasoned answers.	› Sinless › Brought life through sinlessness › Was obedient and brought life to all › Was nailed to a tree (the Cross) but conquered death. › Accept additional reasoned answers.

Eve	Mary
› Eve, a married woman was seduced by a lie. › Eve was seduced by the word of an angel and so fled from God after disobeying His word. › Eve was seduced into disobedience to God › Accept additional reasoned answers.	› Mary, a virgin subject to a husband, undid the evil lie that seduced Eve. › Mary in her turn was given the good news by the word of an angel, and bore God in obedience to His word. › Mary was persuaded into obedience to God › Accept additional reasoned answers.

The fact that God sends His only Son and uses Mary in the way He does in order to correct the wrongs of Adam and Eve and bring about His plan of salvation clearly demonstrates that God continues to love us when we are rejecting Him. Even when man breaks the covenant, God continues to love us.

Teacher Notes

God's Mercy in the Covenant with Noah

LESSON OVERVIEW

Learning Goals

- God offers His mercy through the Holy Catholic Church.
- The Holy Catholic Church is the instrument of salvation.
- The New Testament lies hidden in the Old, and the Old becomes clear in the New.
- God is perfectly just and perfectly merciful.
- God offered His mercy to Noah and his family through an ark, and God continues to offer His mercy through the Church and the Sacraments.

Connection to the Catechism

- CCC 71
- CCC 701
- CCC 845
- CCC 1094
- CCC 1219-1220

Essential Questions

- How is the ark like the Church?
- What is the paradoxical relationship between life and death?

BIBLICAL TOUCHSTONES

For God formed us to be imperishable; the image of his own nature he made us. But by the envy of the devil, death entered the world, and they who are allied with him experience it.

WISDOM 2:23-24

God's patience waited in the days of Noah, during the building of the ark, in which a few, that is, eight persons, were saved through water. Baptism, which corresponds to this, now saves you, not as a removal of dirt from the body but as an appeal to God for a clear conscience, through the resurrection of Jesus Christ, who has gone into heaven and is at the right hand of God, with angels, authorities, and powers subject to him..

1 PETER 3:20-22

The Deluge

BY MICHELANGELO (C. 1508)

C. 1508, fresco, 280 x 570 cm., Sistine Chapel, Vatican.

DIGITAL IMAGES AVAILABLE AT **WWW.SOPHIAINSTITUTEFORTEACHERS.ORG**

Sacred Art and Mercy
The Deluge

The Deluge *(from the ceiling of the Sistine Chapel), Michelangelo, c. 1508*

Directions: Take some time to quietly view and reflect on the art. Let yourself be inspired in any way that happens naturally. Then think about the questions below, and discuss them with your classmates.

Conversation Questions

1. What event has Michelangelo depicted in this fresco?
2. What are some adjectives you would use to describe the action in the scene?
3. Where is the ark?
4. Where is Noah?
5. What does the ark look like?
6. Is the ark in a place of prominence, or is it in the background?
7. Read Genesis 6:5-Genesis 9:17. How does this fresco help you understand the Scripture?

● ES ▲ MS ■ HS

Lesson Plan

Materials

- Sacred Art and Mercy: The Covenant with Noah
- Handout A: Scriptural Foundations
- Handout B: 10 Ways the Ark Prefigured the Church
- Handout C: The Instrument of Salvation, versions 1 and 2
- Handout D: St. Faustina Passage (Diary 1146)

Optional

The following works can be found in the document library at **SophiaInstituteforTeachers.org**:

- *Noah's Ark*, Edward Hicks, 1846
- *Entry of the Animals into Noah's Ark*, Jan Brueghel the Elder, 1613
- *Noah's Ark*, by Franzosischer Meister (The French Master), 1675

Background/Homework

Have students read **Handout A: Scriptural Foundations** and answer the comprehension and critical thinking questions that follow.

Warm-Up

A. Display an image of *The Deluge* from **Sacred Art and Mercy: The Covenant with Noah**. Give students as much time as possible to view the fresco in silence. Allow them to come up to the screen to examine details.

B. Put students in pairs or trios and give each group a laminated color copy of the image. Have students discuss the questions in groups.

Activity

A. After the students have had time to look at and think about the Michelangelo fresco, ask them about its subject.

- Why does the ark look like a church?
- Is the ark in a place of prominence, or is it in the background?

Many will comment that the ark appears in the background. This is true, and herein lies Michelangelo's novel presentation of the Flood. He places the ark in the background. Why? God and righteous living were in the background of people's lives in the days of Noah.

B. Does God and religion remain in the background of people's lives today? And in Michelangelo's day? Where do people turn to be saved?

C. Ask students if they know what is Noah doing in the painting? *His arm is reaching up — towards heaven.*

D. How are the other figures portrayed? *The people left to destruction are focused on themselves in the world, trying to save themselves; they have not lived in God's justice, nor do they truly seek His mercy.*

E. Ask students to describe more familiar depictions of the Flood and Noah's ark. Usually Noah, the ark, the paired animals, the dove of peace, the rainbow, for example, are singularly focused on, without reflection on the justly destructive element of the Flood and the ramifications of what it meant for God to have saved Noah and his family and a numbered portion of creation. How does Michelangelo's image compare and contrast with those depictions?

Wrap-Up

Assign the activity most appropriate for your students' age level:

Read **Handout B: 10 Ways the Ark Prefigured the Church** aloud to younger or middle-grade students while they follow along. Then have them complete the Venn diagram on **Handout C: The Instrument of Salvation**, comparing and contrasting the ark with the Church. Version 1 is blank, and version 2 offers a word bank.

Older students should read **Handout B** independently and then choose one of the following topics and write a reflection essay in response.

- How is Noah like Jesus Christ?
- How is the ark like the Church?
- What is the paradoxical relationship between death and life?
- How does God offer His mercy through the story of Noah and the ark?
- What do the waters of the flood symbolize? How do you know?
- How does the flood signify God's justice? How does the ark signify God's mercy?
- What will God do when He sees His bow set in the clouds, forever?

Enrichment Options

A. Have students consider other depictions of Noah and the ark and compare and contrast them with Michelangelo's *The Deluge*. Look at *Noah's Ark*, by Edward Hicks (1846); *The Entry of the Animals into Noah's Ark*, Jan Brueghel the Elder (1613); and *Noah's Ark*, by

Franzosischer Meister (The French Master; 1675). All of these works are available in the document library at **SophiaInstituteforTeachers.org**.

Hicks's painting is a markedly serene reflection; Brueghel's painting also focuses on the fantastic imagery of the paired animals, gathered alongside Noah's family in peace to enter the boat (unseen, and the skies are clear); The French Master's painting, in contrast to Hicks's and Brueghel's (but similar to Michelangelo's depiction), hints at the import of the impending disaster. Have students break into small groups to compare and contrast the different images of Noah's story. What aspects of the story does each work of art focus on? Which painting do you like most? Which is truest? Which is most beautiful? Groups should share their thoughts and explanations with the class.

B. Have students complete the lesson "The Arks of the Covenants" in the Catholic Curriculum Exchange. The lesson can be found at: **SophiaInstituteforTeachers.org/curriculum/lesson/the-arks-of-the-covenants**. Why do we call the Virgin Mary the Ark of the Covenant?

C. Assign **Handout D: St. Faustina Passage (Diary 1146)** to older students as an essay prompt for reflection to be written in or out of class. The main point of this reflection is to help students see that God offered His mercy to Noah and His family through an ark and that God continues to offer His mercy through the Church and the Sacraments, especially Baptism. Note: *Learn more about St. Faustina in the later lesson "Saints of Mercy."*

HANDOUT A

Scriptural Foundations

Directions: Read the selections and then answer the questions that follow.

Genesis 6:5-Genesis 9:17

The Lord saw that the wickedness of man was great in the earth, and that every imagination of the thoughts of his heart was only evil continually. And the Lord was sorry that he had made man on the earth, and it grieved him to his heart. So the Lord said, "I will blot out man whom I have created from the face of the ground, man and beast and creeping things and birds of the air, for I am sorry that I have made them." But Noah found favor in the eyes of the Lord.

These are the generations of Noah. Noah was a righteous man, blameless in his generation; Noah walked with God. And Noah had three sons, Shem, Ham, and Japheth.

Now the earth was corrupt in God's sight, and the earth was filled with violence. And God saw the earth, and behold, it was corrupt; for all flesh had corrupted their way upon the earth. And God said to Noah, "I have determined to make an end of all flesh; for the earth is filled with violence through them; behold, I will destroy them with the earth. Make yourself an ark of gopher wood; make rooms in the ark, and cover it inside and out with pitch. This is how you are to make it: the length of the ark three hundred cubits, its breadth fifty cubits, and its height thirty cubits. Make a roof for the ark, and finish it to a cubit above; and set the door of the ark in its side; make it with lower, second, and third decks. For behold, I will bring a flood of waters upon the earth, to destroy all flesh in which is the breath of life from under heaven; everything that is on the earth shall die. But I will establish my covenant with you; and you shall come into the ark, you, your sons, your wife, and your sons' wives with you. And of every living thing of all flesh, you shall bring two of every sort into the ark, to keep them alive with you; they shall be male and female. Of the birds according to their kinds, and of the animals according to their kinds, of every creeping thing of the ground according to its kind, two of every sort shall come in to you, to keep them alive. Also take with you every sort of food that is eaten, and store it up; and it shall serve as food for you and for them." Noah did this; he did all that God commanded him.

Genesis 7: The Great Flood

Then the Lord said to Noah, "Go into the ark, you and all your household, for I have seen that you are righteous before me in this generation. Take with you seven pairs of all clean animals, the male and his mate; and a pair of the animals that are not clean, the male and his mate; and seven pairs of the birds of the air also, male and female, to keep their kind alive upon the face of all the earth. For in seven days I will send rain upon the earth forty days and forty nights; and every living thing that I have made I will blot out from the face of the ground." And Noah did all that the Lord had commanded him.

Noah was six hundred years old when the flood of waters came upon the earth. And Noah and his sons and his wife and his sons' wives with him went into the ark, to escape the waters of the flood. Of clean animals, and of animals that are not clean, and of birds, and of everything that creeps on the ground, two and two, male and female, went into the ark with Noah, as God had commanded Noah. And after seven days the waters of the flood came upon the earth.

In the six hundredth year of Noah's life, in the second month, on the seventeenth day of the month, on that day all the fountains of the great deep burst forth, and the windows of the heavens were opened. And rain fell upon the earth forty days and forty nights. On the very same day Noah and his sons, Shem and Ham and Japheth, and Noah's wife and the three wives of his sons with them entered the ark, they and every beast according to its kind, and all the cattle according to their kinds, and every creeping thing that creeps on the earth according to its kind, and every bird according to its kind, every bird of every sort. They went into the ark with Noah, two and two of all flesh in which there was the breath of life. And they that entered, male and female of all flesh, went in as God had commanded him; and the Lord shut him in. The flood continued forty days upon the earth; and the waters increased, and bore up the ark, and it rose high above the earth. The waters prevailed and increased greatly upon the earth; and the ark floated on the face of the waters. And the waters prevailed so mightily upon the earth that all the high mountains under the whole heaven were covered; the waters prevailed above the mountains, covering them fifteen cubits deep. And all flesh died that moved upon the earth, birds, cattle, beasts, all swarming creatures that swarm upon the earth, and every man; everything on the dry land in whose nostrils was the breath of life died. He blotted out every living thing that was upon the face of the ground, man and animals and creeping things and birds of the air; they were blotted out from the earth. Only Noah was left, and those that were with him in the ark. And the waters prevailed upon the earth a hundred and fifty days.

Genesis 8: The Flood Subsides

But God remembered Noah and all the beasts and all the cattle that were with him in the ark. And God made a wind blow over the earth, and the waters subsided; the fountains of the deep and the windows of the heavens were closed, the rain from the heavens was restrained, and the waters receded from the earth continually. At the end of a hundred and fifty days the waters had abated; and in the seventh month, on the seventeenth day of the month, the ark came to rest upon the mountains of Ararat. And the waters continued to abate until the tenth month; in the tenth month, on the first day of the month, the tops of the mountains were seen.

At the end of forty days Noah opened the window of the ark which he had made, and sent forth a raven; and it went to and fro until the waters were dried up from the earth. Then he sent forth a dove from him, to see if the waters had subsided from the face of the ground; but the dove found no place to set her foot, and she returned to him to the ark, for the waters were still on the face of the whole earth. So he put forth his hand and took her and brought her into the ark with him. He waited another seven days, and again he sent forth the dove out of the ark; and the dove came back to him in the evening, and lo, in her mouth a freshly plucked olive leaf; so Noah knew that the waters had subsided from the earth. Then he waited another seven days, and sent forth the dove; and she did not return to him any more.

In the six hundred and first year, in the first month, the first day of the month, the waters were dried from off the earth; and Noah removed the covering of the ark, and looked, and behold, the face of the ground was dry. In the second month, on the twenty-seventh day of the month, the earth was dry. Then God said to Noah, "Go forth from the ark, you and your wife, and your sons and your sons' wives with you. Bring forth with you every living thing that is with you of all flesh – birds and animals and every creeping thing that creeps on the earth – that they may breed abundantly on the earth, and be fruitful and multiply upon the earth." So Noah went forth, and his sons and his wife and his sons' wives with him. And every beast, every creeping thing, and every bird, everything that moves upon the earth, went forth by families out of the ark.

God's Promise to Noah

Then Noah built an altar to the Lord, and took of every clean animal and of every clean bird, and offered burnt offerings on the altar. And when the Lord smelled the pleasing odor, the Lord said in his heart, "I will never again curse the ground because of man, for the imagination of man's heart is evil from his youth; neither will I ever again destroy every living creature as I have done. While the earth remains, seedtime and harvest, cold and heat, summer and winter, day and night, shall not cease."

Genesis 9: The Covenant with Noah

And God blessed Noah and his sons, and said to them, "Be fruitful and multiply, and fill the earth. The fear of you and the dread of you shall be upon every beast of the earth, and upon every bird of the air, upon everything that creeps on the ground and all the fish of the sea; into your hand they are delivered. Every moving thing that lives shall be food for you; and as I gave you the green plants, I give you everything. Only you shall not eat flesh with its life, that is, its blood. For your lifeblood I will surely require a reckoning; of every beast I will require it and of man; of every man's brother I will require the life of man. Whoever sheds the blood of man, by man shall his blood be shed; for God made man in his own image. And you, be fruitful and multiply, bring forth abundantly on the earth and multiply in it."

Then God said to Noah and to his sons with him, "Behold, I establish my covenant with you and your descendants after you, and with every living creature that is with you, the birds, the cattle, and every beast of the earth with you, as many as came out of the ark. I establish my covenant with you, that never again shall all flesh be cut off by the waters of a flood, and never again shall there be a flood to destroy the earth." And God said, "This is the sign of the covenant which I make between me and you and every living creature that is with you, for all future generations: I set my bow in the cloud, and it shall be a sign of the covenant between me and the earth. When I bring clouds over the earth and the bow is seen in the clouds, I will remember my covenant which is between me and you and every living creature of all flesh; and the waters shall never again become a flood to destroy all flesh. When the bow is in the clouds, I will look upon it and remember the everlasting covenant between God and every living creature of all flesh that is upon the earth." God said to Noah, "This is the sign of the covenant which I have established between me and all flesh that is upon the earth."

Comprehension and Critical Thinking Questions

1. According to the Genesis story, why does God destroy mankind with a flood?
2. Whom does God save from the Flood?
3. How does the sacred author describe Noah specifically? How does Noah respond to God's instructions?
4. How did Noah know that the flood waters had subsided and it was safe to depart the ark?
5. What did Noah do first after departing the ark?
6. What promise does God make in his covenant with Noah? What is the sign of this covenant?
7. With whom does God make this covenant – only with Noah's family, or also with all living creatures of flesh on earth, to future generations?
8. How does the Noah story echo the story of Creation?
9. What is Noah's family given the responsibility to do, created and saved two by two, male and female?

HANDOUT B

10 Ways the Ark Prefigured the Church 

by Stephen Beale

When Catholics speak about the Church as the "barque of St. Peter," two images usually come to mind—the actual fishing boat of St. Peter and the ark that saved Noah and his family from the Genesis flood.

Indeed, since the time of the Fathers, Catholics have always seen the epic ark as a type of the Church. Just as the ark was the means by which Noah and his relatives were spared destruction, so also the Church is the instrument by which Christians are saved. The comparison between the two has an explicit biblical foundation in 1 Peter 3, where the apostle writes that the flood itself anticipated the Sacrament of Baptism.

Inspired by Peter and the Genesis account, early Church Fathers elaborated on the many ways in which the ark prefigures the Catholic Church. Here are ten:

Wood and water. Building on the words of 1 Peter 3, St. Augustine argues that the ark represents the primary means of salvation in the New Testament – the wood of the Cross and the waters of Baptism by which Original Sin is washed away (*Contra Faustum*, book XII).

The door on the side. Noah, his family, and the animals all entered the ark through a door on its side (Genesis 6:16). This is analogous to the way we enter the Church through the side of Christ, which was pierced on the Cross, releasing blood and water. "And its having a door made in the side of it certainly signified the wound which was made when the side of the Crucified was pierced with the spear; for by this those who come to Him enter; for thence flowed the sacraments by which those who believe are initiated," Augustine writes in The City of God.

The body of Christ. Even the very ratio of the dimensions of the ark to each other suggest a human body, specifically, the body of Christ, according to Augustine: "For even its very dimensions, in length, breadth, and height, represent the human body in which He came, as it had been foretold. For the length of the human body, from the crown of the head to the sole of the foot, is six times its breadth from side to side, and ten times its depth or thickness, measuring from back to front" (The City of God, book 15).

One ark, one Church. It seems obvious, but the point is a necessary one: there was only one ark, not a fleet of ships or an ark and a few tugboats. Just as there was one ark that saved Noah and his family, so there is one Baptism and one Church. St. Cyprian makes this case in one of his epistles: "The one ark of Noah was a type of the one Church. If, then, in that baptism of the world thus expiated and purified, he who was not in the ark of Noah could be saved by water, he who is not in the Church to which alone baptism is granted, can also now be quickened by baptism."

The decks and stages of the spiritual life. While there was one ark, there were many levels (at least three) within it, which Origen, in his second homily on Genesis, saw as symbolic of the varying progress Christians make in the spiritual life. The fact that there were three itself is noteworthy, as Church tradition often conceives of the spiritual life as progressing in three states: purgative, illuminative, and unitive.

The window above. No detail of the Genesis flood account is insignificant for patristic interpreters such as Augustine. For example, in Genesis 6 we are told that Noah was instructed to make, in addition to the door on the side, an "opening" for daylight, presumably near the top of the ark. Then he was ordered to "finish the ark a cubit about it" (Genesis 6:16). "That the whole ark together is finished in a cubit above; as the Church, the body of Christ gathered into unity, is raised to perfection," St. Augustine writes in *Contra Faustum*.

Penance, the Cross, and Christ. The dimensions of the ark were 300 by 50 by 30 cubits. St. Jerome sees significance in each number. He notes that the Hebrew word for 300 contains a Hebrew letter associated with the cross (because of a prophecy in Ezekiel 9:4), while 50 is a penitential number (because Psalm 50 is penitential in older versions of the Bible such as the Douay-Rheims). Finally, Christ was 30 when He was baptized and began His ministry. In a sense, these three numbers represent the whole compass of the spiritual life: "through penance, we arrive at the mystery of the cross; we reach the mystery of the cross through the perfect Word that is Christ," Jerome concludes in Homily 84 (Early Christian Commentaries on Scripture, InterVarsity Press).

Sealed in love. No nails were used in the construction of the ark. Instead, it was held together by pitch. For Augustine, this symbolizes the way in which the Church is held together by love: "For pitch is a glutinous substance, of great energy and force, to represent the ardor of love which, with great power of endurance, bears all things in the maintenance of spiritual communion" (*Contra Faustum*, Book XII).

Built of saints. The shape of the building material is symbolic too, according to Augustine. "And the fact that it was ordered to be made of squared timbers, signifies the immoveable steadiness of the life of the saints; for however you turn a cube, it still stands," he writes (The City of God, book 15).

God closed the ark. Once Noah, his family, and all the animals are safely in the ark, Genesis 7:16 records this touching detail about who closed the door to the ark: "Then the Lord shut him." (The Greek version of the Old Testament, the Septuagint, adds at the end of the verse: "from the outside.") Church Fathers saw this as an example of God's tender care for men. "Notice in this place too the considerateness in the expression ... to teach us that he had ensured the good man's complete safety," St. John Chrysostom says in his homilies on Genesis (*Early Christian Commentaries on Scripture*).

This essay originally appeared on CatholicExchange.com. It is reprinted here with permission.

HANDOUT C

The Instrument of Salvation

Directions: Complete the Venn diagram, comparing the ark with the Church.

Noah's Ark **The Church**

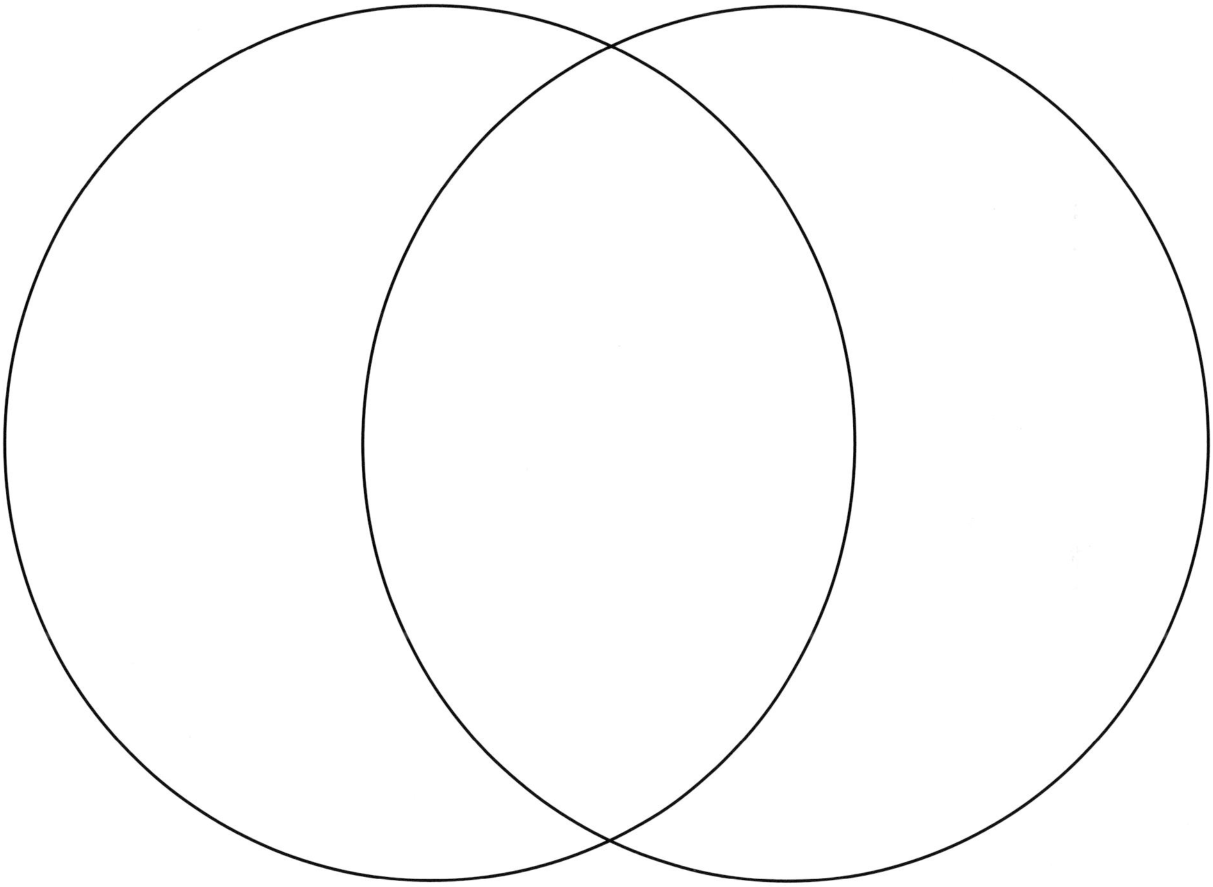

HANDOUT D

The Instrument of Salvation

Directions: Complete the Venn diagram comparing and contrasting the ark with the Church, using phrases from the word bank at the bottom to help you.

Noah's Ark **The Church**

- A place of refuge
- People need(ed) this to be saved
- Saves humanity from sin since Jesus' death and Resurrection
- Saved humanity from death in the Old Testament
- A visible sign of God's mercy
- Built by Noah
- Built by Jesus
- There is only one
- Delivers the righteous to new life
- Held together by pitch
- Held together by love
- God ensures safety for those within it
- The Flood washed away the sins of the world
- Baptism washes away the stain of Original Sin

HANDOUT D

St. Faustina Passage (Diary 1146)

Directions: Read the following quotation from Saint Faustina's Diary. What does the last line mean? What does the last line mean in the context of Noah's time? What does it mean for us today? How do we pass through the door of our Lord's mercy?

1146 (39): Let the greatest sinners place their trust in My mercy. They have the right before others to trust in the abyss of My mercy. My daughter, write about My mercy towards tormented souls. Souls that make an appeal to My mercy delight Me. To such souls I grant even more graces than they ask. I cannot punish even the greatest sinner if he makes an appeal to My compassion, but on the contrary, I justify him in My unfathomable and inscrutable mercy. Write: before I come as a just Judge, I first open wide the door of My mercy. He who refuses to pass through the door of My mercy must pass through the door of My justice.

Answer Key

Sacred Art and Mercy: The Covenant with Noah

1. The Flood
2. Accept reasoned answers.
3. In the background, almost on the horizon
4. Noah is standing in front of the ark, his arms raised heavenward.
5. Accept reasoned answers; students may say the ark looks more like a building than a boat. The ark resembles a church.
6. It is in the background.
7. Accept reasoned answers.

Handout A: Scriptural Foundations

1. The world had become too wicked and corrupt.
2. Noah and his household
3. The Bible describes Noah as righteous and blameless; He walked with God.
4. He sent out a dove which returned to him with an olive leaf in her mouth.
5. He built an altar and offered sacrifices to the Lord.
6. He will never again flood the earth. The sign of the covenant is a rainbow.
7. God makes the covenant with Noah and every living creature for all future generations.
8. Accept reasoned answers.
9. They are charged to be fruitful and multiply, bringing their children forth abundantly.

Handouts C and D: The Instrument of Salvation

Both:

- A place of refuge
- People need(ed) this to be saved
- A visible sign of God's mercy
- There is only one
- Delivers the righteous to new life
- God ensures safety for those within it

The Church:

- Saves humanity from sin since Jesus' death and Resurrection
- Built by Jesus
- Held together by love
- Baptism washes away the stain of Original Sin

The Ark:

- Saved humanity from death in the Old Testament
- Held together by pitch
- Built by Noah
- The Flood washed away the sins of the world

Teacher Notes

The Plan of Mercy Inaugurated: The Covenant with Abraham

LESSON OVERVIEW

Learning Goals

- Abraham is the Father of Faith.
- The promises made to Abraham begin God's plan of salvation.
- The covenant with Abraham is tied to all the other covenants.
- Abraham is a model of faith and trust.
- The sacrifice of Isaac is fulfilled in Christ's sacrifice.
- God's mercy continues to unfold through the covenant with Abraham.

Connection to the Catechism

- CCC 59-61
- CCC 1819

Essential Questions

- What promises did God make to Abraham?
- How are the promises to Abraham fulfilled?
- How do the promises made to Abraham reveal God's mercy to us?

BIBLICAL TOUCHSTONES

The LORD said to Abram: Go forth from your land, your relatives, and from your father's house to a land that I will show you. I will make of you a great nation, and I will bless you; I will make your name great, so that you will be a blessing. I will bless those who bless you and curse those who curse you. All the families of the earth will find blessing in you.

GENESIS 12:1-3

I swear by my very self—oracle of the LORD—that because you acted as you did in not withholding from me your son, your only one, I will bless you and make your descendants as countless as the stars of the sky and the sands of the seashore; your descendants will take possession of the gates of their enemies, and in your descendants all the nations of the earth will find blessing, because you obeyed my command.

GENESIS 22:16-18

The Sacrifice of Isaac
BY CARAVAGGIO (c. 1603)

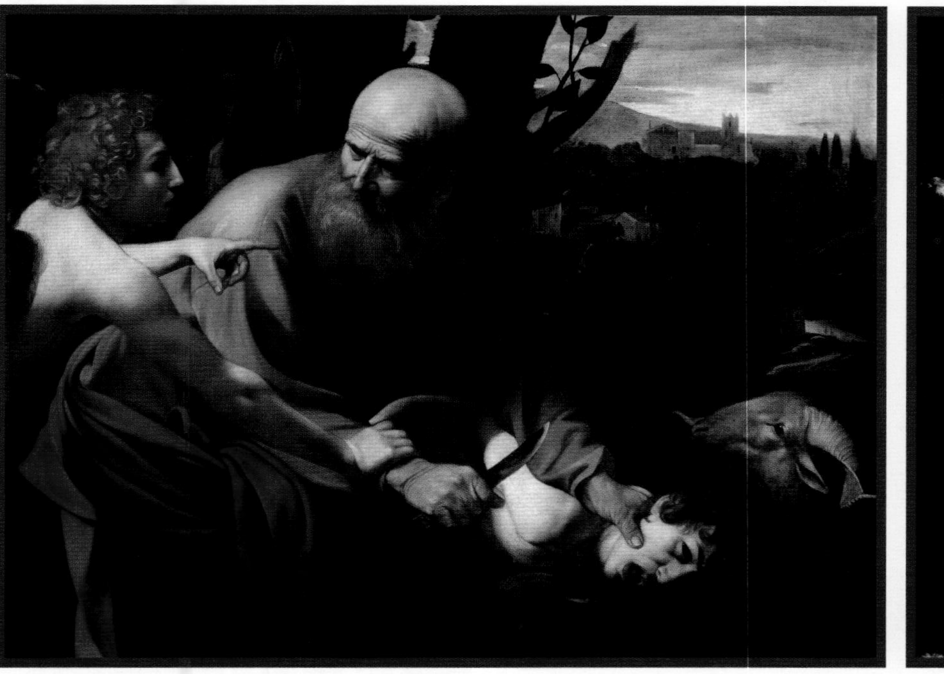

The Sacrifice of Isaac
BY CARAVAGGIO (c. 1617)

DIGITAL IMAGES AVAILABLE AT
WWW.SOPHIAINSTITUTEFORTEACHERS.ORG

Sacred Art and Mercy

The Covenant with Abraham

The Sacrifice of Isaac, *Caravaggio,* c. 1603

Directions: Take some time to quietly view and reflect on the art. Let yourself be inspired in any way that happens naturally. Then think about the questions below, and discuss them with your classmates.

Conversation Questions

1. How does the first painting of *The Sacrifice of Isaac* shown on the left make you feel?
2. What details do you notice that make you feel that way?
3. What would you say is the most intense part of the painting?
4. Who is the man in the painting?
5. Who is the boy whose head the man is holding?
6. Who is the figure on the left?
7. What is the creature on the lower right?
8. Now look at the other depiction of the same event by the same artist. What similarities and differences do you see? Compare and contrast Isaac's facial expressions.
9. The *Catechism of the Catholic Church* calls Abraham the Father of Faith. How is this title fitting in light of these two paintings?
10. Where is the source of light in the paintings? How is each character affected by the light?
11. How do these two paintings depict the faithfulness and mercy of God?

● ES ▲ MS ■ HS

Lesson Plan

Materials

- Sacred Art and Mercy: The Covenant with Abraham
- Handout A: Scriptural Foundations
- Handout B: God's Threefold Promise to Abram
- Teacher Resource: Isaac and Christ Strips
- Handout C: God Keeps His Promises: Isaac and Christ
- Handout D: Abram's Foolish Choice

Background/Homework

A. Have students read **Handout A: Scriptural Foundations** and answer the comprehension and critical thinking questions that follow.

B. Have students bring something from home that is very valuable to them. They may also bring in a photo of the item or person.

Warm-Up I

A. Display an image of the first painting on **Sacred Art and Mercy: The Covenant with Abraham**. Give students as much time as possible to view the painting in silence. Allow them to come up to the screen to examine details. Discuss the questions on the handout as a large group.

B. Display the second painting, and give students time to quietly view it.

C. Put students in pairs or trios and give each group a laminated color copy of **Sacred Art and Mercy: The Covenant with Abraham**. Have students discuss the questions in small groups and then share responses as a large group.

Warm-Up II

A. Go around the room and allow each student to share the item or photo he or she brought and explain why it is special to him or her.

B. Tell students to put their possessions in the middle of the room.

C. Then take out a garbage bag and dramatically unfurl it as you walk toward the pile of items.

D. Inform students you are going to throw them all into the trash. *Variation: Ahead of time, plant a realistic-looking toy cell phone within the items. Hold it up for the class, and then pull a hammer from behind your back and smash the cell phone.*

- How would you feel if I actually did that?
- Would you react differently if God asked you to give up one of those things for Him?
- What if you knew that the sacrifice was going to result in something much better?
- What if God asked you to sacrifice one of your pets? One of your siblings? One of your parents? Could you do it for Him, knowing He had a much bigger plan in mind?
- How do you think Abraham felt when He was asked to sacrifice his only son, Isaac? He was able to do it, yet his idea of God's plan was much less clear than ours.

E. Have students take a moment to write a short reflection essay answering the following question:

- How much do I trust God? Explain.

Activity

A. Spend a few moments reviewing the key events that have taken place in salvation history up to this point:

- Creation
- The Fall
- Cain and Abel
- Noah and the Flood
- The Tower of Babel

B. The promises that God makes to Abraham really begin God's plan of salvation. After Adam broke the covenant at Creation, God promised salvation. Through the Covenant with Noah, God gave humanity a fresh start. With Abraham God really begins unfolding His plan. All the other covenants really are promises being fulfilled to Abraham. Today we are going to explore how that is.

C. Have students complete **Handout B: God's Threefold Promise to Abram**.

D. Review and go over **Handout B**.

E. Ahead of time, copy and cut out the strips on **Teacher Resource: Isaac and Christ Strips**. You'll need enough sets of strips for students working in pairs or trios to receive one set each.

F. Have students use the strips to complete **Handout C: God Keeps His Promises: Isaac and Christ**.

G. After students have had some time to complete the handout, ask them the following questions:

 - How does seeing the connections between the sacrifice of Isaac and the Sacrifice of Christ shed even greater light upon God's mercy and His promises to us?
 - How does knowing this story and how it is fulfilled increase your faith in God and your trust in His mercy?

Wrap-Up

A. As we examine the story of Abraham, it seems that Abraham truly has a tremendous faith. We are correct in making that observation, but Abraham was not perfect. Follow the instructions and complete **Handout D: Abram's Foolish Choice** and discover where he fell short.

B. Conclude by saying the Acts of Faith, Hope, and Love as a class and ask students why these are such fitting prayers to end with after a lesson on Abraham.

Act of Faith

O my God, I firmly believe that you are one God in three divine Persons, Father, Son, and Holy Spirit. I believe that your divine Son became man and died for our sins and that he will come to judge the living and the dead. I believe these and all the truths which the Holy Catholic Church teaches because you have revealed them who are eternal truth and wisdom, who can neither deceive nor be deceived. In this faith I intend to live and die. Amen.

Act of Hope

O Lord God, I hope by your grace for the pardon of all my sins and after life here to gain eternal happiness because you have promised it who are infinitely powerful, faithful, kind, and merciful. In this hope I intend to live and die. Amen.

Act of Love

O Lord God, I love you above all things, and I love my neighbor for your sake because you are the highest, infinite, and perfect good, worthy of all my love. In this love I intend to live and die. Amen.

Extension Options

A. Have students read one of the more controversial parts of this story: Genesis 18:16-33 and Genesis 19:1-29.

B. Spend some time discussing the story based on the following questions:

- What do these passages teach us about prayer and God's mercy?
- To what extent should we ask for mercy not only for ourselves but for others?
- How is God's destroying the cities of Sodom and Gomorrah actually a sign of His mercy and love for the people in those cities?

HANDOUT A

Scriptural Foundations

Directions: Read the selections and then answer the questions that follow.

Genesis 12:1-3

The LORD said to Abram: Go forth from your land, your relatives, and from your father's house to a land that I will show you. I will make of you a great nation, and I will bless you; I will make your name great, so that you will be a blessing. I will bless those who bless you and curse those who curse you. All the families of the earth will find blessing in you.

Genesis 15:1-21

Some time afterward, the word of the LORD came to Abram in a vision: Do not fear, Abram! I am your shield; I will make your reward very great. But Abram said, "Lord GOD, what can you give me, if I die childless and have only a servant of my household, Eliezer of Damascus?" Abram continued, "Look, you have given me no offspring, so a servant of my household will be my heir." Then the word of the LORD came to him: No, that one will not be your heir; your own offspring will be your heir. He took him outside and said: Look up at the sky and count the stars, if you can. Just so, he added, will your descendants be. Abram put his faith in the LORD, who attributed it to him as an act of righteousness. He then said to him: I am the LORD who brought you from Ur of the Chaldeans to give you this land as a possession. "Lord GOD," he asked, "how will I know that I will possess it?" He answered him: Bring me a three-year-old heifer, a three-year-old female goat, a three-year-old ram, a turtledove, and a young pigeon. He brought him all these, split them in two, and placed each half opposite the other; but the birds he did not cut up. Birds of prey swooped down on the carcasses, but Abram scared them away. As the sun was about to set, a deep sleep fell upon Abram, and a great, dark dread descended upon him. Then the LORD said to Abram: Know for certain that your descendants will reside as aliens in a land not their own, where they shall be enslaved and oppressed for four hundred years. But I will bring judgment on the nation they must serve, and after this they will go out with great wealth. You, however, will go to your ancestors in peace; you will be buried at a ripe old age. In the fourth generation your descendants will return here, for the wickedness of the Amorites is not yet complete. When the sun had set and it was dark, there appeared a smoking fire pot and a flaming torch, which passed between those pieces. On that day the LORD made a covenant with Abram, saying: To your descendants I give this land, from the Wadi of Egypt to the Great River, the Euphrates, the land of the Kenites, the Kenizzites, the

Kadmonites, the Hittites, the Perizzites, the Rephaim, the Amorites, the Canaanites, the Girgashites, and the Jebusites.

Genesis 17:1-27

When Abram was ninety-nine years old, the LORD appeared to Abram and said: I am God the Almighty. Walk in my presence and be blameless. Between you and me I will establish my covenant, and I will multiply you exceedingly. Abram fell face down and God said to him: For my part, here is my covenant with you: you are to become the father of a multitude of nations. No longer will you be called Abram; your name will be Abraham, for I am making you the father of a multitude of nations. I will make you exceedingly fertile; I will make nations of you; kings will stem from you. I will maintain my covenant between me and you and your descendants after you throughout the ages as an everlasting covenant, to be your God and the God of your descendants after you. I will give to you and to your descendants after you the land in which you are now residing as aliens, the whole land of Canaan, as a permanent possession; and I will be their God. God said to Abraham: For your part, you and your descendants after you must keep my covenant throughout the ages. This is the covenant between me and you and your descendants after you that you must keep: every male among you shall be circumcised. Circumcise the flesh of your foreskin. That will be the sign of the covenant between me and you. Throughout the ages, every male among you, when he is eight days old, shall be circumcised, including houseborn slaves and those acquired with money from any foreigner who is not of your descendants. Yes, both the houseborn slaves and those acquired with money must be circumcised. Thus my covenant will be in your flesh as an everlasting covenant. If a male is uncircumcised, that is, if the flesh of his foreskin has not been cut away, such a one will be cut off from his people; he has broken my covenant. God further said to Abraham: As for Sarai your wife, do not call her Sarai; her name will be Sarah. I will bless her, and I will give you a son by her. Her also will I bless; she will give rise to nations, and rulers of peoples will issue from her. Abraham fell face down and laughed as he said to himself, "Can a child be born to a man who is a hundred years old? Can Sarah give birth at ninety?" So Abraham said to God, "If only Ishmael could live in your favor!" God replied: Even so, your wife Sarah is to bear you a son, and you shall call him Isaac. It is with him that I will maintain my covenant as an everlasting covenant and with his descendants after him. Now as for Ishmael, I will heed you: I hereby bless him. I will make him fertile and will multiply him exceedingly. He will become the father of twelve chieftains, and I will make of him a great nation. But my covenant I will maintain with Isaac, whom Sarah shall bear to you by this time next year. When he had finished speaking with Abraham, God departed from him.

Then Abraham took his son Ishmael and all his slaves, whether born in his house or acquired with his money—every male among the members of Abraham's household—and he circumcised the flesh of their foreskins on that same day, as God had told him to do. Abraham was ninety-nine years old when the flesh of his foreskin was circumcised, and his son Ishmael was thirteen years old when the flesh of his foreskin was circumcised. Thus, on that same day Abraham and his son Ishmael were circumcised; and all the males of his household, including the slaves born in his house or acquired with his money from foreigners, were circumcised with him.

Genesis 22:1-18

Some time afterward, God put Abraham to the test and said to him: Abraham! “Here I am!” he replied. Then God said: Take your son Isaac, your only one, whom you love, and go to the land of Moriah. There offer him up as a burnt offering on one of the heights that I will point out to you. Early the next morning Abraham saddled his donkey, took with him two of his servants and his son Isaac, and after cutting the wood for the burnt offering, set out for the place of which God had told him. On the third day Abraham caught sight of the place from a distance. Abraham said to his servants: “Stay here with the donkey, while the boy and I go on over there. We will worship and then come back to you.” So Abraham took the wood for the burnt offering and laid it on his son Isaac, while he himself carried the fire and the knife. As the two walked on together, Isaac spoke to his father Abraham. “Father!” he said. “Here I am,” he replied. Isaac continued, “Here are the fire and the wood, but where is the sheep for the burnt offering?” “My son,” Abraham answered, “God will provide the sheep for the burnt offering.” Then the two walked on together. When they came to the place of which God had told him, Abraham built an altar

The Sacrifice of Isaac, Rembrandt van Rijn

there and arranged the wood on it. Next he bound his son Isaac, and put him on top of the wood on the altar. Then Abraham reached out and took the knife to slaughter his son. But the angel of the LORD called to him from heaven, “Abraham, Abraham!” “Here I am,” he answered. “Do not lay your hand on the boy,” said the angel. “Do not do the least thing to him. For now I know that you fear God, since you did not withhold from me your son, your only one.” Abraham looked up and saw a single ram caught by its horns in the thicket. So Abraham went and took the ram and offered it up as a burnt offering in place of his son. Abraham named that place Yahweh-yireh; hence people today say, “On the mountain the LORD will provide.” A second time the angel of the LORD called to Abraham from heaven and said: "I swear by my very self–oracle of the LORD–that because you acted as you did in not withholding from me your son, your only one, I will bless you and make your descendants as countless as the stars of the sky and the sands of the seashore; your descendants will take possession of the gates of their enemies, and in your descendants all the nations of the earth will find blessing, because you obeyed my command."

Comprehension and Critical Thinking Questions

1. What does God promise Abram?
2. What is the significance of God's changing Abram's name to Abraham in chapter 17?
3. Why would God ask Abraham and the men to be circumcised?
4. What does Isaac's name mean? Why does God tell Abraham to name him this?
5. What do these readings teach us about the type of man Abraham was?
6. What insights do these readings give us into who God is?

HANDOUT B

God's Threefold Promise to Abram

Directions: Using the Genesis readings as a reference, answer the following questions and then use the answers to fill in the diagram on the next page.

1. What are the three promises God makes to Abram in Genesis 12:1-3?
2. What promise is God reinforcing and elevating to the level of a covenant in Genesis 15?
3. What covenant later in salvation history fulfills this promise?
4. What promise is God reinforcing and elevating to the level of a covenant in Genesis 17?
5. What covenant later in salvation history fulfills the promise from Genesis 17?
6. What promise is God reinforcing and elevating to the level of a covenant in Genesis 22?
7. What covenant later in salvation history fulfills the promise from Genesis 22?
8. Why does it make sense to say that the promises made to Abraham begin God's plan of salvation?
9. How is God's fulfillment of these promises a sign of His mercy?

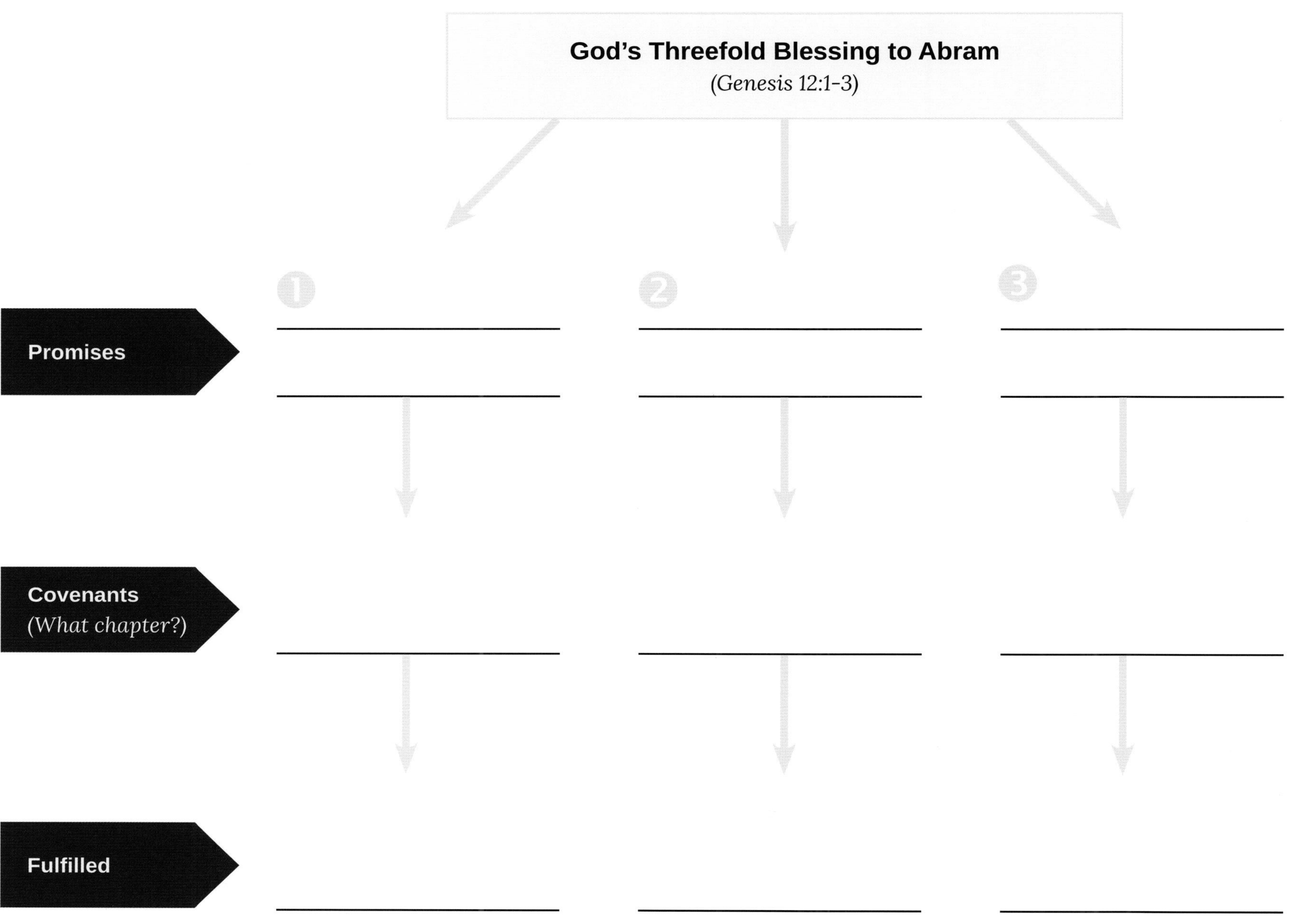
God's Threefold Blessing to Abram
(Genesis 12:1-3)
1
2
3
Promises
Covenants
(What chapter?)
Fulfilled

HANDOUT C

God Keeps His Promises: Isaac and Christ

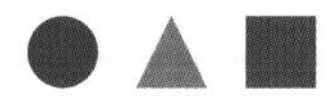

In Scripture, a type is a person or thing in the Old Testament that foreshadows a person or thing in the New Testament. Isaac is a type of Jesus Christ. Complete the chart below by matching the strips showing how Christ fulfills the sacrifice of Isaac. Note any additional connections you see in the space provided. Then answer the questions that follow.

Sacrifice of Isaac	Sacrifice of Christ

Sacrifice of Isaac	Sacrifice of Christ
Additional ways Isaac foreshadows Jesus:	Additional ways Jesus fulfills the sacrifice of Isaac:

1. How does reflecting on the connection between these two sacrifices help you answer the question: "Why would God ask Abraham to sacrifice his son?"

____

____

2. How does knowing the connection between these two sacrifices bring us to a deeper understanding of God's plan for humanity?

____

____

3. How does that understanding lead us to a deeper appreciation of God's mercy?

____

____

TEACHER RESOURCE

Isaac and Christ Strips

Directions: Copy and cut this chart into strips, shuffle the strips, and hand them out in sets to students for them to complete **Handout C**.

Sacrifice of Isaac	Sacrifice of Christ
Abraham offers his beloved son.	God the Father offers up His beloved Son.
Isaac carries the wood for his sacrifice.	Christ carries His wooden Cross.
Isaac's sacrifice takes place on Mount Moriah.	Christ's sacrifice takes place on Golgotha, which is a hill of Mount Moriah.
Isaac submits to Abraham.	Christ submits to the Father and willingly goes to His death.
God provides the sacrifice (a ram).	God provides the sacrifice (Jesus).
On the third day of their journey, Isaac survives the sacrifice.	Jesus conquers death and rises on the third day.
Isaac is bound to the wood of the altar.	Jesus is nailed to a wooden Cross.
Isaac is conceived with divine help.	By the Holy Spirit, Jesus was Incarnate of the Virgin Mary.
Isaac's mother was assured of God's goodness and omnipotence.	Jesus' mother was assured of God's goodness and omnipotence.

Abram's Foolish Choice

Genesis 16:1-6

Abram's wife Sarai had borne him no children. Now she had an Egyptian maidservant named Hagar. Sarai said to Abram: "The LORD has kept me from bearing children. Have intercourse with my maid; perhaps I will have sons through her." Abram obeyed Sarai. Thus, after Abram had lived ten years in the land of Canaan, his wife Sarai took her maid, Hagar the Egyptian, and gave her to her husband Abram to be his wife. He had intercourse with her, and she became pregnant. As soon as Hagar knew she was pregnant, her mistress lost stature in her eyes. So Sarai said to Abram: "This outrage against me is your fault. I myself gave my maid to your embrace; but ever since she knew she was pregnant, I have lost stature in her eyes. May the LORD decide between you and me!" Abram told Sarai: "Your maid is in your power. Do to her what you regard as right." Sarai then mistreated her so much that Hagar ran away from her.

The Angel Appears to Hagar and Ishmael, Guercino

Genesis 21:9-21

Sarah noticed the son whom Hagar the Egyptian had borne to Abraham playing with her son Isaac; so she demanded of Abraham: "Drive out that slave and her son! No son of that slave is going to share the inheritance with my son Isaac!" Abraham was greatly distressed because it concerned a son of his. But God said to Abraham: Do not be distressed about the boy or about your slave woman. Obey Sarah, no matter what she asks of you; for it is through Isaac that descendants will bear your name. As for the son of the slave woman, I will make a nation of him also, since he too is your offspring. Early the next morning Abraham got some bread and a skin of water and gave them to Hagar. Then, placing the child on her back, he sent her away. As she roamed aimlessly in the wilderness of Beer-sheba, the water in the skin was used up. So she put the child down under one of the bushes, and then went and sat down opposite him, about a bowshot away; for she said to herself, "I cannot watch the child die." As she sat opposite him, she wept aloud. God heard the boy's voice, and God's angel called to Hagar from heaven: "What is the matter, Hagar? Do not fear; God has heard the boy's voice in this plight of his. Get up, lift up the boy and hold him by the hand; for I will make of him a great nation." Then God opened her eyes, and she saw a well of water. She went and filled the skin with water, and then let the boy drink.

God was with the boy as he grew up. He lived in the wilderness and became an expert bowman. He lived in the wilderness of Paran. His mother got a wife for him from the land of Egypt.

Comprehension and Critical Thinking Questions

1. What mistake does Abram make?
2. What are some of the consequences of that action?
3. Putting this story in context with the other sections we have read and discussed, how is God merciful to Abram with this situation?
4. How can God's mercy be found within the consequences?
5. How have you experienced God's mercy in the midst of a difficult situation that was a result of a bad decision you made?

Answer Key

Handout B: God's Threefold Promise to Abram

1. Land or nation, name or dynasty, and a worldwide blessing
2. Land or nation
3. Covenant with Moses/Mosaic covenant
4. Name or dynasty
5. Covenant with David/Davidic covenant
6. Worldwide blessing
7. New Covenant in Christ
8. Every covenant that follows is a result of a promise made to Abraham.
9. Throughout the rest of salvation history, and even in the midst of this very story, God experiences various levels of rejection from His people due to sin and idolatry. Despite all these things, God remains faithful. He continues to love even when that love is rejected. Accept additional reasoned answers

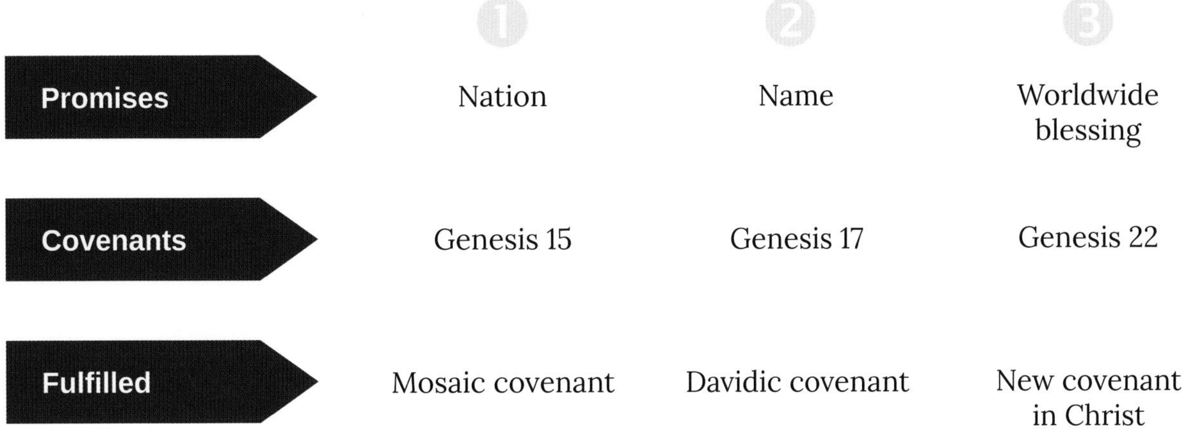

Handout C: God Keeps His Promises: Isaac and Christ

Note: Use the original teacher resource page as a key to match up the strips.

1. Accept reasoned answers.
2. Accept reasoned answers.
3. Accept reasoned answers.

Handout D: Abram's Foolish Choice

1. He has relations with his maidservant at his wife's prompting in order to have a child with her.
2. Abram's relationship with Sarai is strained; Hagar looks on Sarai with contempt; Sarai beats Hagar; Hagar runs away; Abram ends up sending Hagar and Ishmael away; Abram disappoints God.
3. God continues to be by Abraham's side and reveal his plan; eventually Sarah gives birth to Isaac; God remains faithful to His promises and fulfills them; Abraham eventually does have descendants as numerous as the stars through Isaac's line; accept additional reasoned answers.
4. Consequences are often the way God can intervene and get us to pay attention. A consequence can often lead us to avoid making the same mistake again. Accept additional reasoned answers.
5. Accept reasoned answers.

God's Mercy Tested: The Covenant with Moses

LESSON OVERVIEW

Learning Goals

- Moses was an intercessory figure and a covenant mediator.
- God's mercy is present in the promises of the covenant.
- The Ten Commandments constitute the terms of the covenant.
- God's Chosen People tested the covenant.

Connection to the Catechism

- CCC 62
- CCC 72
- CCC 204-213
- CCC 2574-2577

Essential Questions

- How is Moses an intercessory figure for God's covenant with the Chosen People?
- How is God's mercy evident in the Exodus story?
- How did the Israelites test God's mercy?

BIBLICAL TOUCHSTONES

The Israelites ate the manna for forty years, until they came to settled land; they ate the manna until they came to the borders of Canaan.

EXODUS 16:35

Your ancestors ate the manna in the desert, but they died; this is the bread that comes down from heaven so that one may eat it and not die. I am the living bread that came down from heaven; whoever eats this bread will live forever; and the bread that I will give is my flesh for the life of the world.

JOHN 6:49

Promulgatio Legis Scripte per Moisem

BY COSIMO ROSSELLI (1481–1482)

1481–1482, fresco, 350 x 72 cm, Sistine Chapel, Vatican

DIGITAL IMAGES AVAILABLE AT

WWW.SOPHIAINSTITUTEFORTEACHERS.ORG

Sacred Art and Mercy

The Covenant with Moses

Promulgatio Legis Scripte per Moisem, *Cosimo Rosselli, 1481–1482*

Directions: Take some time to quietly view and reflect on the art. Let yourself be inspired in any way that happens naturally. Then think about the questions below, and discuss them with your classmates.

Conversation Questions

1. A fresco is a painting done on wet plaster. This fresco is in the Sistine Chapel. Where is the Sistine Chapel?
2. Can you find Moses in this fresco? Why do you think Moses appears in it more than once? Does this fresco depict one event or many?
3. The fresco is sometimes called *The Descent from Mount Sinai*. What important event happened on Mount Sinai?
4. Find Moses receiving the tablets of the Law from God. What is the significance of Moses' receiving these tablets? Read Exodus 24:12-17 and 31:18. How does this fresco help you understand these verses?
5. Read Exodus 32:1-6 and summarize what is happening. Can you find this event depicted in the fresco?
6. Does it seem hard to believe that the Israelites would worship a golden calf? Do people today treat non-holy things as though they were sacred? If so, give some examples.
7. When God told Moses what the people were doing, what was Moses' response?
8. Read Exodus 34:1-5. Can you find this scene in the fresco?
9. In what ways does this fresco show us Moses as the intercessory figure between God and His Chosen People?
10. How do all the scenes in this fresco taken together show us God's mercy?

● ES ▲ MS ■ HS

Lesson Plan

Materials

- Holy Bible
- *Catechism of the Catholic Church*
- Sacred Art and Mercy: The Covenant with Moses
- Handout A: Scriptural Foundations
- Handout B: Moses' Extraordinary Life
- Teacher Resource: Timeline of Moses' Life
- Handout C: Analyzing the Covenant
- Paper, watercolor paint, and paintbrushes

Background/Homework

Have students read the book of Exodus to become acquainted with Moses' life, the Exodus of the Chosen People, God's covenant with the Chosen People, their disobedience, and God's mercy. They should familiarize themselves especially with the selections on **Handout A: Scriptural Foundations**.

Warm-Up I

A. Ask students to close their eyes as you read aloud Exodus 24:12-17. When you have finished, read it a second time, this time as a visualization exercise. Ask students to imagine the scene from the perspective of the Israelites and of Moses. Why does this event look different to each of them?

B. Invite students to connect what happens in these verses to other parts of the Bible. For example, connect God's speaking to Moses on the seventh day to the days of Creation and the Sabbath rest; Moses stays atop Mount Sinai for forty days, the number of days of rain during the Flood and of Jesus' fast in the desert.

C. Display an image of the Cosimo Rosselli fresco *Promulgatio Legis Scripte per Moisem* (*Promulgation of the Written Law through Moses*). This image is on **Sacred Art and Mercy: The Covenant with Moses**. Give students as much time as possible to view the image in silence. Allow them to come up to the screen to examine details.

D. Put students in pairs or trios and give each group a laminated color copy of the handout. Have students discuss the questions in groups and then share responses as a large group.

Warm-Up II

A. Distribute **Handout B: Moses' Extraordinary Life** and go over his story.

B. In a mini-lecture, review the three themes of mercy, covenant, and intercessory figure:

God's covenants with man are great signs of His mercy toward us. All God's covenants with man have basic components.

- *a covenant* ***mediator****; in this case, it is Moses.*
- ***promises*** *that accompany the covenant; in this case, it is the Promised Land of milk and honey.*
- ***terms*** *of the covenant; in this case, there are the Ten Commandments written by God and given to Moses on Mount Sinai.*
- *the* ***sign*** *by with the covenant is remembered; in this case, it is the Passover meal.*
- *the type of* ***family*** *that God has a result of the covenant; in this case, it is the nation of Israel.*

Moses is the covenant mediator, and as such he is the intercessory figure between the Chosen People and God.

Activity

A. Students should take out their Bibles and copies of the *Catechism of the Catholic Church*. Distribute **Handout C: Analyzing the Covenant** and read over the Bible passages and Catechism paragraphs.

B. Students should then categorize each passage according to its emphasis on God's mercy, the covenant, or the intercessory figure.

C. When students have finished, dialogue about their choices.

D. Point out that although these passages emphasize either mercy, the covenant, or the intercessor, frequently they are all part of an integrated whole. The covenant itself is an act of divine mercy and requires an intercessor. Moses was the intercessor for the Israelites; Christ is both God and the intercessor for the New and Everlasting Covenant.

Wrap-Up

Give students a large piece of blank paper and make watercolor paints available. Invite students to select an event from Moses' life and draw or paint it from the perspective of Moses on one half of the paper and from the perspective of the Israelites on the other half.

Alternatively, they may choose several episodes from his life and paint them in the style of the Rosselli fresco.

Extension

The same artist painted Christ delivering the Beatitudes, using a similar composition and style. A digital copy of *Sermon on the Mount* can be found at **SophiaInstituteforTeachers.org**. Have students compare and contrast these two paintings, insofar as they teach us about the covenants and mercy. For example:

- Both the Ten Commandments and the Beatitudes are given to the people through divine revelation.
- The Ten Commandments were given to the Chosen People; the Beatitudes are offered to all of humanity.
- Moses was a human mediator; Christ is God who became man.
- The Ten Commandments consist mainly of things we must not do; the Beatitudes teach us what we must do.

Sermon on the Mount, Cosimo Rosselli

HANDOUT A

Scriptural Foundations

Directions: Read the following quotations from the book of Exodus.

Exodus 3:7-8

"But the LORD said: I have witnessed the affliction of my people in Egypt and have heard their cry against their taskmasters, so I know well what they are suffering. Therefore I have come down to rescue them from the power of the Egyptians."

Exodus 3:14-15

"God replied to Moses: I am who I am. Then he added: This is what you will tell the Israelites: I AM has sent me to you. God spoke further to Moses: This is what you will say to the Israelites."

Exodus 12:14

"This day will be a day of remembrance for you, which your future generations will celebrate with pilgrimage to the LORD; you will celebrate it as a statute forever."

Exodus 16:3-4

"The Israelites said to them, 'If only we had died at the LORD's hand in the land of Egypt, as we sat by our kettles of meat and ate our fill of bread! But you have led us into this wilderness to make this whole assembly die of famine!' Then the LORD said to Moses: I am going to rain down bread from heaven for you. Each day the people are to go out and gather their daily portion; thus will I test them, to see whether they follow my instructions or not."

Exodus 24:7-8

"Taking the book of the covenant, he read it aloud to the people, who answered, "All that the LORD has said, we will hear and do." Then he took the blood and splashed it on the people, saying, "This is the blood of the covenant which the LORD has made with you according to all these words."

Exodus 34:6

"So the LORD passed before him and proclaimed: The LORD, the LORD, a God gracious and merciful, slow to anger and abounding in love and fidelity."

Exodus 34:10

"The LORD said: Here is the covenant I will make. Before all your people I will perform marvels never before done in any nation anywhere on earth, so that all the people among whom you live may see the work of the LORD. Awe-inspiring are the deeds I will perform with you!"

Come to class next time prepared to discuss the following:

- How is Moses an intercessory figure for God's covenant with the Chosen People?
- How is God's mercy evident in the Exodus story?
- What are the conditions and promises set forth by God's covenant with Moses?
- What is the sign by which the covenant will be remembered?
- How did the Israelites test God's mercy?

HANDOUT B

Moses' Extraordinary Life

From 1700 B.C. to 1280 B.C. (Book of Exodus)

1. Since the death of Joseph around 1700 B.C., the 12 tribes of Israel suffered 420 years of slavery in Egypt under the harsh rule of many pharaohs.
2. The Jews were growing so numerous that they began to threaten to outnumber the Egyptians. Around the time of the birth of Moses, the pharaoh decreed that all newborn male Hebrews were to be killed.
3. To save Moses' life, his mother put the three-month-old Moses into a reed basket and hid the basket among the reeds in the Nile River.
4. Pharaoh's daughter found Moses in the river. She retrieved him, adopted him, and raised him.
5. When he became a man, Moses killed an Egyptian who was too harsh with a Hebrew. He had to flee Egypt to avoid facing the pharaoh's wrath. He went to Midian.
6. Moses stayed many years in Midian and eventually married Zipporah, one of the seven daughters of a priest of Midian.
7. God spoke to Moses through the burning bush on Mount Horeb. Moses was sent on a mission to Egypt to command that pharaoh let the Israelites go out of Egypt.
8. Pharaoh refused, and God brought 10 plagues down on the Egyptian people. The 10th plague was the death of all firstborn children and animals who did not have the Passover sign of a lamb's blood on their doorp osts and lintels.
9. After Pharaoh's firstborn son died, he agreed to let Moses' people go.
10. Moses led the Israelites out of Egypt. Pharaoh changed his mind and pursued them into the desert to slaughter them. God parted the Red Sea and the Israelites were able to walk through it to escape.

From 1280 B.C. to 1240 B.C. (Books of Numbers, and Deuteronomy): Forty Years of Wandering in the Sinai Desert

1. The Israelites wandered in the Sinai desert for 40 years because of their failure to believe and trust in God.
2. God cared for the Israelites by providing daily manna in the morning and quail at night; He also gave them strict dietary rules.
3. Moses went up to Mount Sinai, where he encountered God. God gave him the Ten Commandments and the instructions for building the Ark of the Covenant (Exodus 25:10-16).
4. God guaranteed Moses that He would keep the promises He made to Abraham.
5. God gave the command that the Ark of the Covenant had to be placed at the center of the tabernacle in the tent of the Holy of Holies.
6. God gave the laws to the Israelites, who were His Chosen People.

Moses Breaking the Tablets of the Law, by Rembrandt Harmenszoon van Rijn

7. The Israelites were thirsty. God commanded Moses and Aaron to command a rock to bring forth water. Moses instead struck the rock twice with his staff, saying, "Just listen, you rebels! Are we to produce water for you out of this rock?" (Numbers 20:10). Water ran out of the rock so that the Israelites and their livestock could drink.
8. Moses died and was buried before the Chosen People entered the Promised Land.

Timeline of Moses' Life

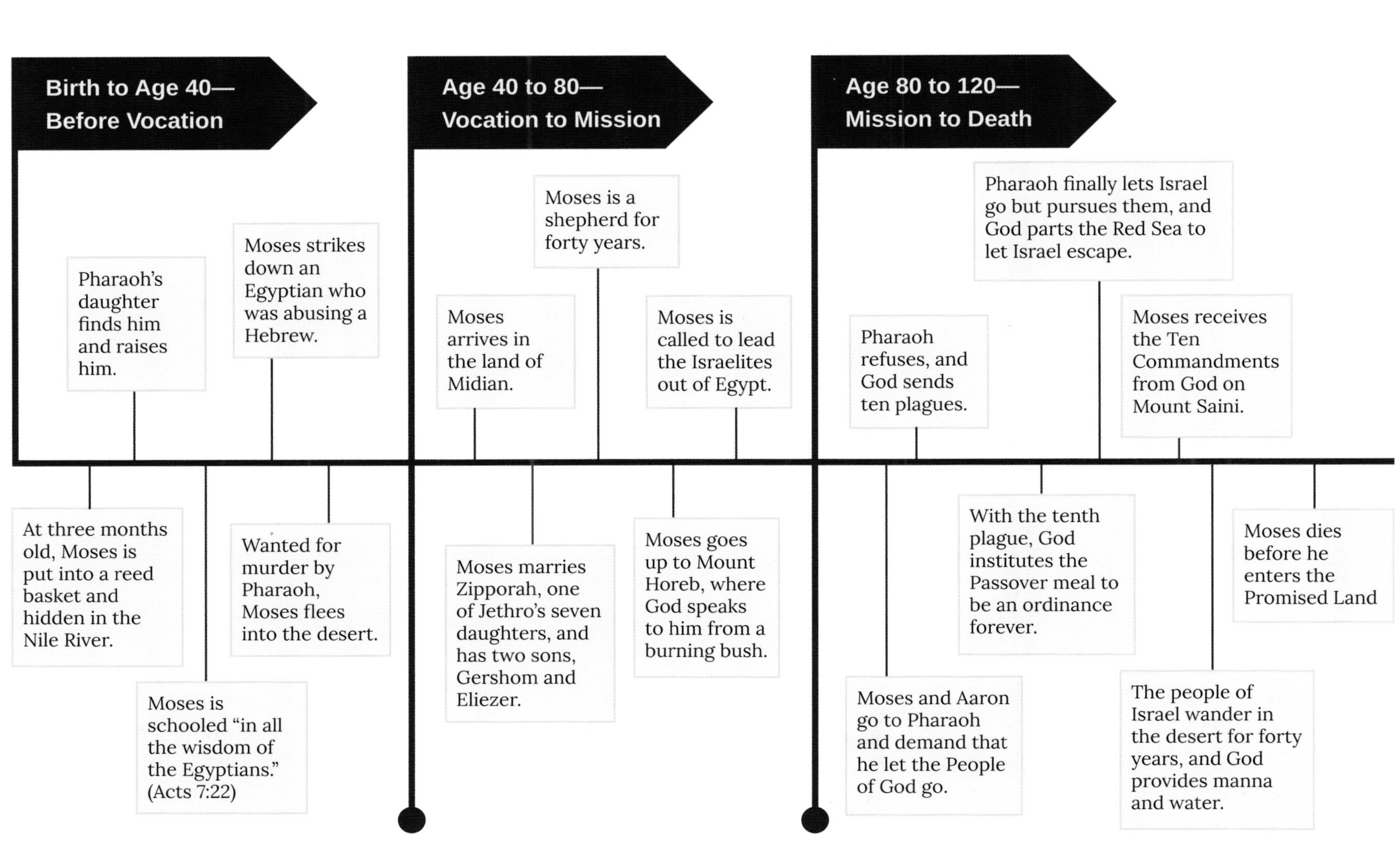

HANDOUT C

Analyzing the Covenant

Directions: Look up and read the following Bible passages and *Catechism of the Catholic Church* paragraphs that illustrate God's mercy, the concept of the covenant, and the role of Moses as an intercessory figure. Then use them to fill in the chart by putting them into their proper category.

- **Exodus 34:6**
- **Exodus 12:14**
- **CCC 2576**
- **Exodus 3:7**
- **Exodus 3:14**
- **Exodus 34:10**
- **CCC 2574**
- **CCC 62**
- **Exodus 16:3-4**

Covenant	Mercy	Intercessory Figure

Answer Key

Sacred Art and Mercy: The Covenant with Moses

1. The Sistine Chapel is in the Apostolic Palace, the residence of the Pope in Vatican City, Rome.
2. The man with the long white beard is Moses. The fresco depicts several events.
3. Moses received the Ten Commandments from God.
4. Moses would be the mediator between God and His Chosen People. After freeing them from slavery in Egypt, God gave His people the Law so they would be able to keep their gift of new life.
5. The Israelites are upset that Moses has been delayed, and they think they need a new god to worship. Aaron gathers up their gold and produces a golden calf. The people worship the calf.
6. Accept reasoned answers, but guide students to the conclusion that in today's world people often make idols of non-holy things, such as money, material possessions, celebrities, politicians, and so forth, by making these things the center of their lives. When we do this, we are giving these things the reverence that we should show only to God.
7. Moses asked God to show the people mercy, and God "changed his mind about the punishment he had threatened to inflict on His people" (Exodus 32:14). Moses broke the tablets of the Law (Exodus 32:19). Later, Moses offered his own life in atonement for the Israelites' sin (Exodus 32:32).
8. This scene is depicted in the background on the right.
9. Moses intercedes for his people by asking God to show them mercy when they sin.
10. God continues to love His people despite their rejection of Him, and He gives them new chances to return to communion with Him.

Handout C: Analyzing the Covenant

Answers may vary. Accept reasoned responses as to the integrated nature of all the quotations. Below are suggested responses.

Mercy: Exodus 3:7; 16:3-4; 34:6

Covenant: Exodus 12:14; 34:10; CCC 62

Intercessory Figure: Exodus 3:14; CCC 2574; CCC 2576

Teacher Notes

God's Mercy Persists: The Covenant with David

LESSON OVERVIEW

Learning Goals

- Mercy is conveyed by the Latin word *misericordia*, which denotes the misery of man's condition redeemed by the mercy of God's heart.
- David is an example of a true penitent.
- God's mercy has no limits.
- We are all in need of God's mercy.

Connection to the Catechism

- CCC 1081, 1481, 2538
- CCC 2578-2580

Essential Questions

- What is *misericordia*?
- How does God honor David? How does He punish David?
- How does David exemplify true penitence?

BIBLICAL TOUCHSTONES

My sacrifice, O God, is a contrite spirit; a contrite, humbled heart, O God, you will not scorn.

PSALMS 51:19

Those preceding him as well as those following kept crying out: "Hosanna! Blessed is he who comes in the name of the Lord! Blessed is the kingdom of our father David that is to come! Hosanna in the highest!"

MARK 11:9-10

Voronet Monastery, Romania (detail of painted exterior walls)

ARTIST UNKNOWN (C. 1547)

C. 1547

DIGITAL IMAGES AVAILABLE AT
WWW.SOPHIAINSTITUTEFORTEACHERS.ORG

Sacred Art and Mercy

Voronet Monastery, Romania (detail of painted exterior walls)

Voronet Monastery, Romania *(detail of painted exterior walls)*, c. 1547

Directions: Take some time to quietly view and reflect on the art. Let yourself be inspired in any way that happens naturally. Then think about the questions below, and discuss them with your classmates.

Conversation Questions

1. This image comes from a fresco painted on the exterior wall of a monastery in Romania. Do you know where Romania is?
2. What stands out to you about this fresco? What are your favorite parts?
3. What questions would you have for the artist?
4. Because of its many interior and exterior paintings, Voroneț Monastery has come to be known as the Sistine Chapel of the East. What is the Sistine Chapel? Why do you think this monastery has earned this nickname?
5. King David is holding a lyre, an instrument similar to a harp. Why would he be pictured holding this instrument? (Hint: see 1 Samuel 16:18 and 16:23.)
6. This detail is from a larger painting of the Last Judgment. David was a notorious sinner. How is it possible, then, that he is pictured with a halo?

● ES ▲ MS ■ HS

Lesson Plan

Materials

- Sacred Art and Mercy: The Covenant with David
- Handout A: Scriptural Foundations
- Handout B: Psalm 51 in Latin and English
- Teacher Resource A: Mini-Lecture Notes on Allegri's Miserere
- YouTube video: Allegri's *Miserere* **www.youtube.com/watch?v=YDOENZediM8**
- Handout C: Covenants, Mercy, and Justice in David, Peter, and Judas
- Teacher Resource B: A Guide to *Lectio Divina*

Background/Homework

Have students read **Handout A: Scriptural Foundations** for homework. In addition to reading, they should list all the moral mistakes that David makes in this one short reading. Note: 1. *David should not have been on the roof in Jerusalem; he should have been in battle with his men. 2. He should not have lingered and entertained his desire for Bathsheba. 3. He should not have lain with Bathsheba. 4. He should not have tried to cover his misdeed and disguise Bathsheba's pregnancy (by intoxicating Uriah and trying to get him to go home to his wife to lie with her). 5. David should not have had Uriah killed in battle.*

Warm-Up I

A. Display an image of the painting on **Sacred Art and Mercy: The Covenant with David**. Give students as much time as possible to view the fresco in silence. Allow them to come up to the screen to examine details. Discuss the questions on the handout as a large group.

B. Put students in pairs or trios and give each group a laminated color copy of the painting. Have students discuss the questions in groups and then share their responses as a large group.

Warm-Up II

A. Review homework reading assignment and hear from students what moral mistakes by David they identified. Ensure that they understand David's moral failure, Nathan's parable, and God's punishment.

B. Ask the students if David was repentant. Was David contrite for his sins? Students should be able to provide evidence of David's contrition. Define the word *contrition: sorrow of the soul and hatred for the sin committed, together with a resolution not to sin again.* Contrition is the most important act of the penitent and is necessary for the reception of the Sacrament of Penance (CCC 1451).

C. Tell the students that David composed a prayer, Psalm 51, after Nathan helped him realize his sin. Distribute **Handout B: Psalm 51 in Latin and English** and read it aloud.

D. After students have read through Psalm 51, ask the following questions:

- Does David seem contrite? More, less, or the same as you thought before?
- Does it make sense that Psalm 51 mentions purity and blood-guilt?
- You may wish to clarify for students that 51:5 does not mean that the marital act is sinful. Rather, David is lamenting the stain of Original Sin and the fact that his entire life has been afflicted by sin.
- Can David's prayer apply to more people than just David? Can anyone sincerely pray Psalm 51? Can you and I?

E. Introduce Allegri's *Miserere* with **Teacher Resource A: Mini-Lecture Notes on Allegri's *Miserere***. Play the piece from YouTube: **www.youtube.com/watch?v=YDOENZediM8**.

Activity

A. Break students into groups and have them discuss the figures of David, Peter, and Judas. What were the sins of each figure? How did they seek God's mercy?

B. Working together, have students complete **Handout C: Covenants, Mercy, and Justice in David, Peter, and Judas**.

C. After students have had a chance to complete the handout, take time to go over the answers, emphasizing the different results of these figures' actions, especially in terms of mercy.

Wrap-Up

A. Arrange for a time for students to receive the Sacrament of Confession. As a preparation, invite the students to meditate on Psalm 51 using Lectio Divina. See **Teacher Resource B: A Guide to *Lectio Divina***.

B. If Confession is not available, a meditation on Psalm 51 can still be done, or conclude by saying Psalm 51 slowly aloud together.

HANDOUT A

Scriptural Foundations

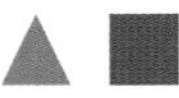

Directions: Read the selections from the Holy Bible. Afterward, make a list of all the moral mistakes made by David.

2 Samuel 11

In the spring of the year, the time when kings go forth to battle, David sent Joab, and his servants with him, and all Israel; and they ravaged the Ammonites, and besieged Rabbah. But David remained at Jerusalem. It happened, late one afternoon, when David arose from his couch and was walking upon the roof of the king's house, that he saw from the roof a woman bathing; and the woman was very beautiful. And David sent and inquired about the woman. And one said, "Is not this Bathsheba, the daughter of Eliam, the wife of Uriah the Hittite?" So David sent messengers, and took her; and she came to him, and he lay with her. (Now she was purifying herself from her uncleanness.) Then she returned to her house. And the woman conceived; and she sent and told David, "I am with child." So David sent word to Joab, "Send me Uriah the Hittite." And Joab sent Uriah to David. When Uriah came to him, David asked how Joab was doing, and how the people fared, and how the war prospered. Then David said to Uriah, "Go down to your house, and wash your feet." And Uriah went out of the king's house, and there followed him a present from the king. But Uriah slept at the door of the king's house with all the servants of his lord, and did not go down to his house. When they told David, "Uriah did not go down to his house," David said to Uriah, "Have you not come from a journey? Why did you not go down to your house?" Uriah said to David, "The ark and Israel and Judah dwell in booths; and my lord Joab and the servants of my lord are camping in the open field; shall I then go to my house, to eat and to drink, and to lie with my wife? As you live, and as your soul lives, I will not do this thing." Then David said to Uriah, "Remain here today also, and tomorrow I will let you depart." So Uriah remained in Jerusalem that day, and the next. And David invited him, and he ate in his presence and drank, so that he made him drunk; and in the evening he went out to lie on his couch with the servants of his lord, but he did not go down to his house. In the morning David wrote a letter to Joab, and sent it by the hand of Uriah. In the letter he wrote, "Set Uriah in the forefront of the hardest fighting, and then draw back from him, that he may be struck down, and die." And as Joab was besieging the city, he assigned Uriah to the place where he knew there were valiant men. And the men of the city came out and fought with Joab; and some of the servants of David among the people fell. Uriah the Hittite was slain also. Then Joab sent and told David all the news about the fighting; and he instructed the messenger, "When you have finished telling all the news about the fighting to the king, then, if the king's anger rises, and if he says to you, 'Why did you go so near the city to fight? Did you not know that they would shoot from the wall? Who killed Abimelech the son of Jerubbesheth? Did not a woman cast an upper millstone upon him from the wall, so that he died at Thebez? Why did you go so near the wall?' then you shall say, 'Your servant Uriah the Hittite is dead also.'" So the messenger went, and came and told David all that Joab had sent him to tell. The messenger said to David, "The men gained an advantage over us, and came out against us in the field; but we drove them back to the entrance of the gate. Then the archers shot at your servants from the wall; some of the king's servants are dead; and your servant Uriah the Hittite is dead also." David said to the messenger, "Thus shall you say to Joab, 'Do not let this matter trouble you, for the sword devours now one and now another; strengthen your attack upon the city, and overthrow it.' And encourage him." When the wife of Uriah heard that Uriah her husband was dead, she made lamentation for her husband. And when the mourning was over, David sent and brought her to his house, and she became his wife, and bore him a son. But the thing that David had done displeased the LORD.

2 Samuel 12

And the LORD sent Nathan to David. He came to him, and said to him, "There were two men in a certain city, the one rich and the other poor. The rich man had very many flocks and herds; but the poor

King David Giving Uriah a Letter, Giovanni Francesco Barbieri, Il Guercino

man had nothing but one little ewe lamb, which he had bought. And he brought it up, and it grew up with him and with his children; it used to eat of his morsel, and drink from his cup, and lie in his bosom, and it was like a daughter to him. Now there came a traveler to the rich man, and he was unwilling to take one of his own flock or herd to prepare for the wayfarer who had come to him, but he took the poor man's lamb, and prepared it for the man who had come to him." Then David's anger was greatly kindled against the man; and he said to Nathan, "As the LORD lives, the man who has done this deserves to die; and he shall restore the lamb fourfold, because he did this thing, and because he had no pity." Nathan said to David, "You are the man. Thus says the LORD, the God of Israel, 'I anointed you king over Israel, and I delivered you out of the hand of Saul; and I gave you your master's house, and your master's wives into your bosom, and gave you the house of Israel and of Judah; and if this were too little, I would add to you as much more. Why have you despised the word of the LORD, to do what is evil in his sight? You have smitten Uriah the Hittite with the sword, and have taken his wife to be your wife, and have slain him with the sword of the Ammonites. Now therefore the sword shall never depart from your house, because you have despised me, and have taken the wife of Uriah the Hittite to be your wife.' Thus says the LORD, 'Behold, I will raise up evil against you out of your own house; and I will take your wives before your eyes, and give them to your neighbor, and he shall lie with your wives in the sight of this sun. For you did it secretly; but I will do this thing before all Israel, and before the sun.'" David said to Nathan, "I have sinned against the LORD." And Nathan said to David, "The LORD also has put away your sin; you shall not die. Nevertheless, because by this deed you have utterly scorned the LORD, the child that is born to you shall die." Then Nathan went to his house. And the LORD struck the child that Uriah's wife bore to David, and it became sick. David therefore besought God for the child; and David fasted, and went in and lay all night upon the ground. And the elders of his house stood beside him, to raise him from the ground; but he would not, nor did he eat food with them. On the seventh day the child died. And the servants of David feared to tell him that the child was dead; for they said, "Behold, while the child was yet alive, we spoke to him, and he did not listen to us; how then can we say to him the child is dead? He may do himself some harm." But when David saw that his servants were whispering together, David perceived that the child was dead; and David said to his servants, "Is the child dead?" They said, "He is dead." Then David arose from the earth, and washed, and anointed himself, and changed his clothes; and he went into the house of the LORD, and worshiped; he then went to his own house; and when he asked, they set food before him, and he ate. Then his servants said to him, "What is this thing that you have done? You fasted and wept for the child while it was alive; but when the child died, you arose and ate food." He said, "While the child was still alive, I fasted and wept; for I said, 'Who knows whether the LORD will be gracious to me, that the child may live?' But now he is dead; why should I fast? Can I bring him back again? I shall go to him, but he will not return to me."

David's Moral Failures

1. ____

____

2. ____

____

3. ____

____

4. ____

____

5. ____

____

How many can you identify?

2 – Good!

3 – Great!

4 – Excellent!

5 – Doctor of Moral Theology!

Reflection Questions

1. What is contrition?
2. How does God honor David? Why does God honor David?
3. How does God punish David? Why does God punish David?
4. What can Nathan's parable to King David tell us about ourselves?
5. What is King David's role in receiving God's mercy?

HANDOUT B

Psalm 51 in Latin and English

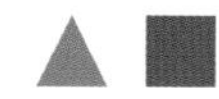

Miserere mei, Deus

Miserere mei, Deus: secundum magnam misericordiam tuam.

Et secundum multitudinem miserationum tuarum, dele iniquitatem meam.

Amplius lava me ab iniquitate mea: et a peccato meo munda me.

Quoniam iniquitatem meam ego cognosco: et peccatum meum contra me est semper.

Tibi soli peccavi, et malum coram te feci: ut justificeris in sermonibus tuis, et vincas cum judicaris.

Ecce enim in iniquitatibus conceptus sum: et in peccatis concepit me mater mea.

Ecce enim veritatem dilexisti: incerta et occulta sapientiae tuae manifestasti mihi.

Asperges me hysopo, et mundabor: lavabis me, et super nivem dealbabor.

Audi tui meo dabis gaudium et laetitiam: et exsultabunt ossa humiliata.

Averte faciem tuam a peccatis meis: et omnes iniquitates meas dele.

Cor mundum crea in me, Deus: et spiritum rectum innova in visceribus meis.

Ne proiicias me a facie tua: et spiritum sanctum tuum ne auferas a me.

Redde mihi laetitiam salutaris tui: et spiritu principali confirma me.

Docebo iniquos vias tuas: et impii ad te convertentur.

Have mercy on me, O God

Have mercy on me, God, in accord with your merciful love;

in your abundant compassion blot out my transgressions.

Thoroughly wash away my guilt; and from my sin cleanse me.

For I know my transgressions; my sin is always before me.

Against you, you alone have I sinned; I have done what is evil in your eyes

So that you are just in your word, and without reproach in your judgment.

Behold, I was born in guilt, in sin my mother conceived me.

Behold, you desire true sincerity; and secretly you teach me wisdom.

Cleanse me with hyssop, that I may be pure; wash me, and I will be whiter than snow.

You will let me hear gladness and joy; the bones you have crushed will rejoice.

Turn away your face from my sins; blot out all my iniquities.

A clean heart create for me, God; renew within me a steadfast spirit.

Do not drive me from before your face, nor take from me your holy spirit.

Restore to me the gladness of your salvation; uphold me with a willing spirit.

Libera me de sanguinibus, Deus, Deus salutis meae: et exsultabit lingua mea justitiam tuam.

Domine, labia mea aperies: et os meum annuntiabit laudem tuam.

Quoniam si voluisses sacrificium, dedissem utique: holocaustis non delectaberis.

Sacrificium Deo spiritus contribulatus: cor contritum, et humiliatum, Deus, non despicies.

Benigne fac, Domine, in bona voluntate tua Sion: ut aedificentur muri Ierusalem.

Tunc acceptabis sacrificium justitiae, oblationes, et holocausta: tunc imponent super altare tuum vitulos.

I will teach the wicked your ways, that sinners may return to you.

Rescue me from violent bloodshed, God, my saving God, and my tongue will sing joyfully of your justice.

Lord, you will open my lips; and my mouth will proclaim your praise.

For you do not desire sacrifice or I would give it; a burnt offering you would not accept.

My sacrifice, O God, is a contrite spirit; a contrite, humbled heart, O God, you will not scorn.

King David in Prayer, Pieter de Grebber

TEACHER RESOURCE A

Mini-Lecture Notes on Allegri's *Miserere*

Gregorio Allegri (1582-1652) was an Italian priest and composer of the Roman School of composers. Allegri's masterpiece was composed in 1638 for an annual Tenebrae celebration during Holy Week. Two times during Holy Week, on Wednesday and Friday at a 3:00 a.m. service, twenty-seven candles were put out one at a time until there remained a single lit candle. It was said that the Holy Father would participate in these services. Allegri composed the Miserere to be performed at the end of the Tenebrae services, and the pope would kneel and pray at the altar with the single remaining burning candle. This must have been a holy, solemn, beautiful moment to behold.

There were many versions of the *Miserere* written, first by Costanzo Festa as early as 1518. Ten more composers, including Guerrero and Palestrina, proffered their own versions of this sorrowful psalm, but Allegri's stirring rendition overshadowed the rest until it became the only rendition used, and it remains with us today. It became such a prized possession of Holy Mother Church that there was a prohibition of its performance outside the Sistine Chapel, and under the pain of excommunication it was forbidden to copy it. Nonetheless, by 1770 there were at least three copies known to exist, one by Padre Giovanni Battista Martini (1706-1784), one held by the king of Portugal, and another copy said to be housed in the Imperial Library in Vienna.

Throughout the years there have been many intriguing stories concerning its performances and journeys. However, none is quite as compelling as the story of a twelve-year-old Mozart. In December of 1769, Leopold and Wolfgang Mozart left their hometown of Salzburg for a fifteen-month tour of Italy. There they came across none other than Padre Giovanni Martini, known for having taught Johann Christian Bach. Young Wolfgang went to Bologna to be taught by Padre Giovanni as well. In April of 1770, the Mozarts visited St. Peter's Basilica to celebrate the Wednesday Tenebrae. They wanted to hear the famous Miserere performed at the Sistine Chapel. The youthful Mozart was so moved by the Miserere that when he returned to his accommodations that evening, he wrote out the entire manuscript from memory. On Good Friday, he went to the service to hear it again and make minor corrections to his manuscript. Wolfgang's father, Leopold, wrote of this achievement to his wife on April, 14, 1770, from Rome:

> *You have often heard of the famous* Miserere *in Rome, which is so greatly prized that the performers are forbidden on pain of excommunication to take away a single part of it, copy it, or to give it to anyone. But we have it already.*

> *Wolfgang has written it down, and we would have sent it to Salzburg in this letter, if it were not necessary for us to be there to perform it. But the manner of performance contributes more to its effect than the composition itself. Moreover, as it is one of the secrets of Rome, we do not wish to let it fall into other hands.*

There is a mysterious twist to the end of this tale. It turns out that Mozart's manuscript of the Miserere has never been found, and it can be supposed that it would have been very informative concerning the style and creativeness employed by the papal choir in 1771. However, there is a famous music historian named Dr. Charles Burney who made a tour of Italy around the same time Mozart returned to study with Padre Martini. Although we know practically nothing of the interaction, Dr. Burney met with Wolfgang in Bologna with Padre Martini. When Dr. Burney returned from his tour, he published a collection of music used during Holy Week in the Sistine Chapel, and included was a rendition of Allegri's Miserere. Since then it has been copied many times and in many places.

Allegri's *Miserere* remains one of the most recorded pieces of music in Church history and after listening to it several times, it is easy to see why. It is a haunting call to repentance in recognition of the misery of human frailty in the face of God's call to sanctity. It calls one to contemplate the chasm between the misery of man and the heart of God. We can listen to this and ponder God's mercy toward sinners. Mercy is conveyed by the Latin word *misericordia* – denoting the misery of man's condition redeemed by the mercy of God's heart. Listening to Allegri's *Miserere* and contemplating the Latin word for *mercy* can help clarify the relationship between our duty to confess and repent of our miserable conditions as the means to cooperate with God's gift of His own heart by His unfathomable and undeserved mercy.

HANDOUT C

Covenants, Mercy, and Justice in David, Peter, and Judas

Directions: Using the reading on David and a Holy Bible, complete this table based on the moral failures and outcomes of the biblical figures David, Peter, and Judas Iscariot. Refer to the Scripture verses and a Holy Bible if you need a reminder of the stories.

Scripture	Figure	Sin	Result
2 Samuel 7:1-17; 2 Samuel 11-12:23			
Mathew 26:34; Mark 14:30; Luke 22:61, 62; Matthew 16:18-19			
Mark 14:10-72			

A Guide to *Lectio Divina*

Lectio Divina, meaning "divine reading," refers to a kind of meditation by which one reads very slowly and prayerfully a spiritual writing such as verses from Holy Scripture or the writings of the saints. It is distinct from vocal prayer and contemplation. *The Catechism of the Catholic Church* explains:

2708 Meditation engages thought, imagination, emotion, and desire. This mobilization of faculties is necessary in order to deepen our convictions of faith, prompt the conversion of our heart, and strengthen our will to follow Christ. Christian prayer tries above all to meditate on the mysteries of Christ, as in *lectio divina* or the rosary. This form of prayerful reflection is of great value, but Christian prayer should go further: to the knowledge of the love of the Lord Jesus, to union with him.

Lectio divina, as a kind of meditation, incorporates many pauses for reflection. Certain words or phrases will catch one's thought and imagination. Interior repetition is common in *lectio divina*, as are interior tangents when one explores the application of certain words to one's life. Other words and phrases of the text may be passed over much more quickly, for they do not catch the mind on this particular occasion for prayer. Next time, they may resound. One's meditation would never be identical to another's, nor would it be identical for the same person at another time. Thus, good spiritual writing provides an inexhaustible source for meditation on the mysteries of the Catholic Faith.

For this exercise, each student should hold a copy of Psalm 51 for silent prayer either in the classroom or in a chapel. This is an individual, personal, quiet type of prayer.

Answer Key

Handout C: Covenants, Mercy, and Justice in David, Peter, and Judas

Scripture	Figure	Sin	Result
2 Samuel 7:1-17; 2 Samuel 11-12:23 Covenant, David's transgression and repentance	David	Lowly shepherd called to kingship by God; reaps many gifts in God's favor and covenant; greatly displeases God by taking Bathsheba and slaying Uriah to have her	Nathan enlightens David to his sin and David repents; his first son by Bathsheba is taken in punishment, but God honors their covenant and restores David, whose Son will be the Savior, Jesus
Mathew 26:34; Mark 14:30; Luke 22:61, 62; Matthew 16:18-19 Peter's denial and role in the Church	Peter	Humble disciple of Jesus, devoted, loving, and faithful, but denies his Master in fear	Receives forgiveness and trusts in mercy; receives the keys to the Kingdom, leads and teaches in Christ's saving Church, extending God's mercy to sinners
Mark 14:10-72 Judas betrays Jesus	Judas	Judas, one of the twelve Apostles, betrays Jesus for money	Despairs instead of trusting in mercy, hangs himself and exemplifies strict justice: sin has its consequence/punishment; lack of humility and contrition on the sinner's part

God's Plan for Mercy Comes to Fulfillment: The New Covenant in Christ

LESSON OVERVIEW

Learning Goals

- Jesus Christ is the fullness of all revelation.
- Through His public ministry, Jesus Christ teaches us about mercy and how to extend mercy to others.
- Jesus reveals the fullness and depths of His mercy through the Paschal Mystery.
- The mercy of Christ is infinite and is always available to us, no matter what.

Connection to the Catechism

- CCC 65-67
- CCC 430-455
- CCC 571-594

Essential Questions

- In what ways can we see God's love and mercy fully revealed in Jesus Christ?
- How are you in need of God's mercy?
- How is God calling you to show mercy to someone else?
- How can you respond to that call?

BIBLICAL TOUCHSTONES

For the Son of Man did not come to be served but to serve and to give his life as a ransom for many.

MARK 10:45

In the beginning was the Word, and the Word was with God, and the Word was God. He was in the beginning with God. All things came to be through him, and without him nothing came to be. What came to be through him was life, and this life was the light of the human race; the light shines in the darkness, and the darkness has not overcome it. And the Word became flesh and made his dwelling among us, and we saw his glory, the glory as of the Father's only Son, full of grace and truth.

JOHN 1:1-5, 14

The Woman at the Well

ANGELICA KAUFFMAN (1796)

1796, oil on canvas, 123.5 x 1585 cm., Neue Pinakothek, Munich, Germany.

DIGITAL IMAGES AVAILABLE AT

WWW.SOPHIAINSTITUTEFORTEACHERS.ORG

Sacred Art and Mercy
The Woman at the Well

The Woman at the Well, *Angelica Kauffman, 1796*

Directions: Take some time to quietly view and reflect on the art. Let yourself be inspired in any way that happens naturally. Then think about the questions below, and discuss them with your classmates.

Conversation Questions

1. What words or phrases come to mind when you first look at this image?
2. What event is depicted in this painting?
3. What message does Jesus' posture communicate?
4. Look at the woman's posture and facial expression. What do you think she is thinking or wanting to say?
5. Why do you think both Jesus and the woman are wearing red? Do Christ and the woman look similar in any other ways? Why do you think the artist chose to paint them that way?
6. Read the story in John 4:4-42. Why is it significant that the woman is a Samaritan? How did the Jews regard Samaritans?
7. Does the Samaritan woman have to tell Jesus everything about herself, or does He already know? What is His reaction?
8. Why is this exchange between Jesus and the Samaritan woman known as the Water of Life discourse? Who or what is the water of life?
9. How is the Samaritan woman transformed by her encounter with Christ?
10. How is the story that is memorialized in this painting a great summary of salvation history and God's mercy?

● ES ▲ MS ■ HS

Lesson Plan

Materials

- Sacred Art and Mercy: The Woman at the Well
- Handout A: Scriptural Foundations
- Handout B: The Magnificat
- Handout C: Gospel Scavenger Hunt
- Poster board or butcher paper and markers
- Handout D: Reflecting on Jesus' Mercy

Background/Homework

Have students read **Handout A: Scriptural Foundations** and answer the questions that follow.

Warm-Up I

A. Display an image of the painting on **Sacred Art and Mercy: The Woman at the Well**. Give students as much time as possible to view the painting in silence. Allow them to come up to the screen to examine details. Discuss the questions on the handout as a large group.

B. Put students in pairs or trios and give each group a laminated color copy of the painting. Have students discuss the questions in groups and then share responses as a large group.

Warm-Up II

A. Begin class by giving students a copy of **Handout B: The Magnificat**. Explain to students that this is Mary's prayer after the Annunciation.

B. Read/pray the prayer together as a class.

C. After you have read the prayer, pose the following questions to students:

- Based on what you know about the rest of salvation history, what is so significant about the words Mary speaks here?
- How does Mary recognize the fullness of God's mercy before anyone else?
- How does Mary serve as a model of what it means to be a disciple of mercy?

Activity

A. Begin by writing "Jesus fulfills all covenants" and "Jesus is the fullness of mercy" on the board.

B. Then go around the room and ask students to name as many examples from the Gospels as they can think of that exemplify either or both of these statements. Write down their answers on the board around the phrases. You may want to ask a student to be the recorder.

C. Break the students up into four groups. Assign each group one of the four Gospels.

D. Have each group complete **Handout C: Gospel Scavenger Hunt**.

E. After students have had some time to complete **Handout C**, hand out large pieces of butcher paper or poster board and markers to each group.

F. Have each group summarize their findings from the handout in a creative or artistic way.

G. Have each group present their poster and information to the class. Hang the posters up around the room after the presentations and give students time to view them all.

Wrap-Up

A. Play the YouTube video of nonviolent flashback scenes from *The Passion of the Christ*. It can be accessed at **www.youtube.com/watch?v=l7v5bWzx4yE**.

B. After watching the video, ask the students to close their eyes and listen prayerfully as you read Luke 23.

C. As you conclude the reading of the chapter from the Gospel, move into praying a decade of the Rosary as a class. Pray the Fifth Sorrowful Mystery: the Crucifixion.

D. Pass out **Handout D: Reflecting on Jesus' Mercy** and have students complete it quietly and prayerfully. You may want to play some quiet meditative music as they work on it.

Scriptural Foundations

Directions: Read the selection and answer the questions that follow.

Acts 2:14-41

Then Peter stood up with the Eleven, raised his voice, and proclaimed to them, "You who are Jews, indeed all of you staying in Jerusalem. Let this be known to you, and listen to my words. These people are not drunk, as you suppose, for it is only nine o'clock in the morning. No, this is what was spoken through the prophet Joel: 'It will come to pass in the last days,' God says, 'that I will pour out a portion of my spirit upon all flesh. Your sons and your daughters shall prophesy, your young men shall see visions, your old men shall dream dreams. Indeed, upon my servants and my handmaids I will pour out a portion of my spirit in those days, and they shall prophesy. And I will work wonders in the heavens above and signs on the earth below: blood, fire, and a cloud of smoke. The sun shall be turned to darkness, and the moon to blood, before the coming of the great and splendid day of the Lord, and it shall be that everyone shall be saved who calls on the name of the Lord.' You who are Israelites, hear these words. Jesus the Nazorean was a man commended to you by God with mighty deeds, wonders, and signs, which God worked through him in your midst, as you yourselves know. This man, delivered up by the set plan and foreknowledge of God, you killed, using lawless men to crucify him. But God raised him up, releasing him from the throes of death, because it was impossible for him to be held by it. For David says of him:

'I saw the Lord ever before me, with him at my right hand I shall not be disturbed. Therefore my heart has been glad and my tongue has exulted; my flesh, too, will dwell in hope, because you will not abandon my soul to the netherworld,

St. Peter Preaching in the Presence of St. Mark, Bl. Fra Angelico

nor will you suffer your holy one to see corruption. You have made known to me the paths of life; you will fill me with joy in your presence.' My brothers, one can confidently say to you about the patriarch David that he died and was buried, and his tomb is in our midst to this day. But since he was a prophet and knew that God had sworn an oath to him that he would set one of his descendants upon his throne, he foresaw and spoke of the resurrection of the Messiah, that neither was he abandoned to the netherworld nor did his flesh see corruption. God raised this Jesus; of this we are all witnesses. Exalted at the right hand of God, he received the promise of the holy Spirit from the Father and poured it forth, as you [both] see and hear. For David did not go up into heaven, but he himself said: 'The Lord said to my Lord, "Sit at my right hand until I make your enemies your footstool."' Therefore let the whole house of Israel know for certain that God has made him both Lord and Messiah, this Jesus whom you crucified." Now when they heard this, they were cut to the heart, and they asked Peter and the other apostles, "What are we to do, my brothers?" Peter [said] to them, "Repent and be baptized, every one of you, in the name of Jesus Christ for the forgiveness of your sins; and you will receive the gift of the holy Spirit. For the promise is made to you and to your children and to all those far off, whomever the Lord our God will call." He testified with many other arguments, and was exhorting them, "Save yourselves from this corrupt generation." Those who accepted his message were baptized, and about three thousand persons were added that day.

Reflection Questions

1. This passage from Acts is the first time Peter preaches after Pentecost. What are the main points of his exhortation?
2. What effect does his exhortation have on the people? What does this tell us about the power of Christ and His mercy?
3. How is this an appropriate summary of everything discussed in this book?
4. How does this passage call us to respond to Christ?

Reflect on these questions for next class:

5. How does Jesus fulfill all covenants?
6. How is the whole of Jesus' life, death, and Resurrection directed toward extending mercy toward humanity?
7. How does Jesus call us to receive His mercy and then extend that mercy to others?

HANDOUT B

The Magnificat

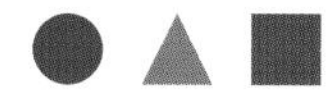

Directions: Read Luke 1:46-55, below.

And Mary said:

"My soul proclaims the greatness of the Lord;
my spirit rejoices in God my savior.
For he has looked upon his handmaid's lowliness;
behold, from now on will all ages call me blessed.
The Mighty One has done great things for me,
and holy is his name.

His mercy is from age to age
to those who fear him.
He has shown might with his arm,
dispersed the arrogant of mind and heart.

He has thrown down the rulers from their thrones
but lifted up the lowly.
The hungry he has filled with good things;
the rich he has sent away empty.

He has helped Israel his servant,
remembering his mercy,
according to his promise to our fathers,
to Abraham and to his descendants forever."

HANDOUT C

Gospel Scavenger Hunt

Directions: Search your assigned Gospel to find examples of each of the following. Be sure to include chapter, verse, and quotations and/or a summary of the content. After completing the scavenger hunt, answer the three questions at the end. Then raise your hand to receive instructions for the next part of the activity.

1. Find two examples of Jesus healing someone physically.

____

____

2. Find one example of Jesus performing an exorcism or casting out demons.

____

____

3. Find two examples of Jesus publicly forgiving the sins of someone.

____

____

4. Find two examples of Jesus doing something that exemplifies humility or saying something about the importance of being humble.

____

____

5. Find a reference to the Eucharist.

6. Find two examples of Jesus challenging others to be merciful.

7. How do all of these examples reveal the mercy of Christ in some way?

8. What does every single one of these passages tell us about who Jesus is and what He desires for each of us?

9. Based on these passages, how is it appropriate to say that Jesus reveals to us the fullness of God's mercy?

HANDOUT D

Reflecting on Jesus' Mercy

Directions: Spend some time reflecting and journaling on the following questions.

1. How did all the scenes in the video reflect the tenderness and mercy of God? Which scene moved you the most? Why?

2. What is an image or moment from the reading of the Gospel passage that stood out most to you? Why?

3. How does reflecting on Jesus' Passion allow us to realize the depths of His mercy? How are you in need of God's mercy in your life? How can you respond to that need?

____

____

____

____

____

____

____

____

4. How is God calling you to show mercy to someone else? How can you respond to that call?

____

____

____

____

____

____

____

____

Exploring the Corporal and Spiritual Works of Mercy with Sacred Art ● ▲

LESSON OVERVIEW

Learning Goal

- Jesus gives us a model for living the Corporal and Spiritual Works of Mercy.

Connection to the Catechism

- CCC 2447

Essential Questions

- Why did Jesus wash the disciples feet?
- Should we understand the words wash and clean only in their literal sense?
- How does Jesus wash us and make us clean?

BIBLICAL TOUCHSTONES

[N]ot because of any righteous deeds we had done but because of His mercy, He saved us through the bath of rebirth and renewal by the Holy Spirit.

TITUS 3:5

He came to Simon Peter, who said to him, "Master, are you going to wash my feet?" Jesus answered and said to him, "What I am doing, you do not understand now, but you will understand later." Peter said to him, "You will never wash my feet." Jesus answered him, "Unless I wash you, you will have no inheritance with me." Simon Peter said to him, "Master, then not only my feet, but my hands and head as well."

JOHN 13:6-9

Jesus Washing Peter's Feet

BY FORD MADOX BROWN (1856)

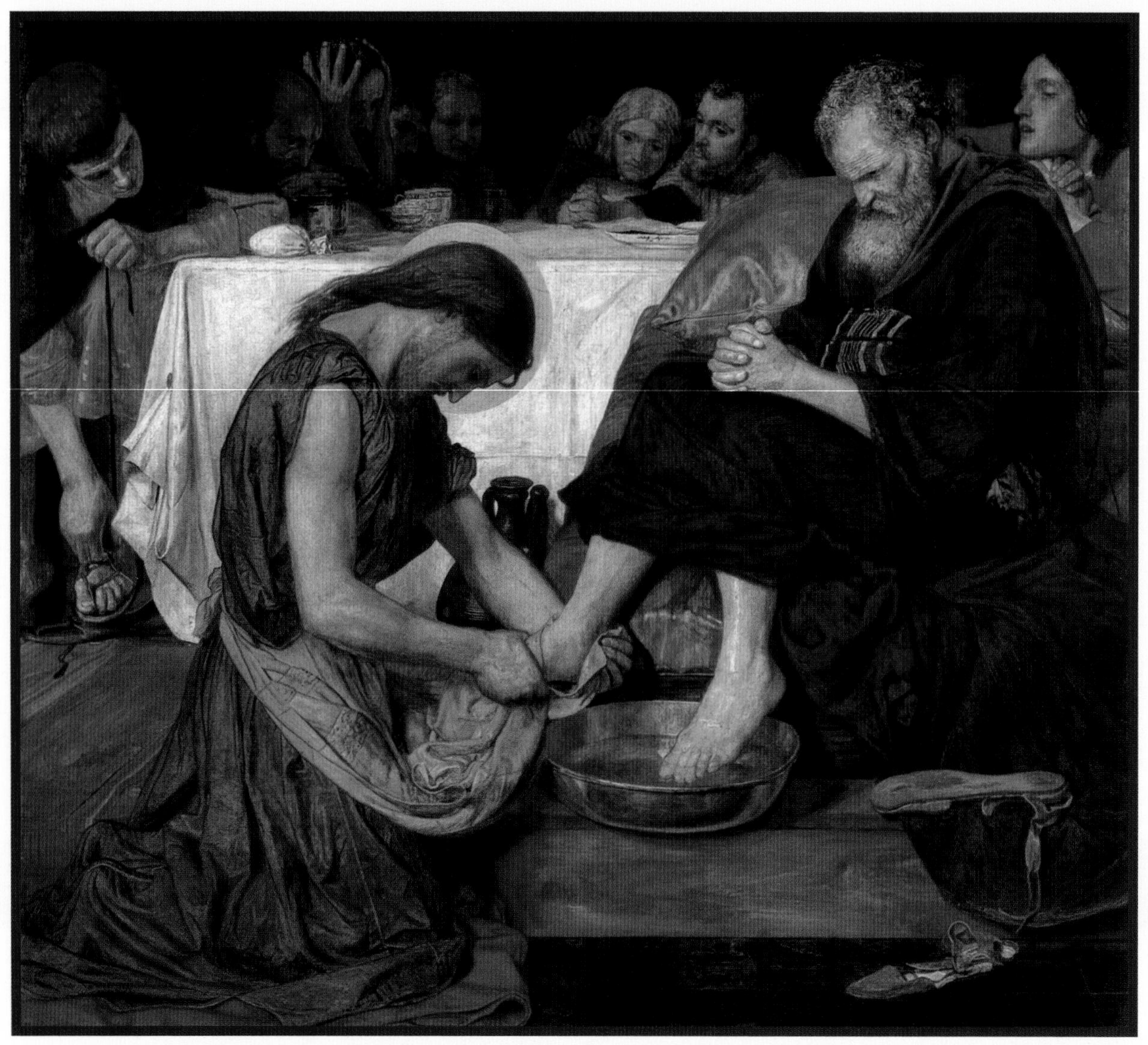

Oil paint on canvas. City of Manchester Art Galleries, Manchester, UK.

DIGITAL IMAGES AVAILABLE AT
WWW.SOPHIAINSTITUTEFORTEACHERS.ORG

Sacred Art and Mercy
Jesus Washing Peter's Feet

Jesus Washing Peter's Feet, *Ford Madox Brown, 1856*

Directions: Take some time to quietly view and reflect on the art. Let yourself be inspired in any way that happens naturally. Then think about the questions below, and discuss them with your classmates.

Conversation Questions

1. Who is the man kneeling?
2. What is He doing?
3. Who is the man whose feet are being washed?
4. Who are the people in the background? Where does this scene take place?
5. What event in the Bible does this painting show us?
6. Read John 13:1-20. How does this painting help you understand these verses?
7. Why is Peter surprised that Jesus would wash his feet?
8. How does Jesus respond to Peter's surprise?
9. What does Jesus tell the disciples in verses 14-15? What are some things He models in this Gospel?
10. Should we understand the words wash and clean in these verses in a strictly literal sense? In other words, might they mean something else in addition to their ordinary meanings? How does Jesus "wash" us? How does He make us "clean"?

ES MS

Lesson Plan

Materials

- Sacred Art and Mercy: The Corporal and Spiritual Works of Mercy
- Handout A: Foot Washing

Warm-Up I

A. Display an image of *Jesus Washing Peter's Feet* by Ford Madox Brown. This image is on **Sacred Art and Mercy: The Corporal and Spiritual Works of Mercy**. Give students as much time as possible to view the painting in silence. Allow them to come up to the screen to examine details.

B. Once several minutes have passed, ask students:

- What do you first notice about this work of art?
- What do you like about this work of art?
- How does this work of art make you feel?
- How do the colors in the work of art draw your eye?
- What is happening in this picture?

Warm-Up II

Give students a little background on the practice of foot washing; for example:

- In ancient times, having your guests' feet washed was a way to show them honor.
- Foot washing was commonly practiced in desert climates, where sandals were the usual footwear.
- In these climates, water was rare and precious, yet gracious hosts offered it to their guests.
- The lowest servant in the household was expected to wash the feet of guests.

Activity

A. Put students in small groups and give each group a laminated copy of **Sacred Art and Mercy: The Corporal and Spiritual Works of Mercy**. Have them discuss the questions on the back of the handout with each other. During this time, focus on keeping students intent on the artwork and the discussion questions, letting their conversations go in unexpected ways.

B. Display the image on **Handout A: Foot Washing**. Ask students to compare this image with the Brown painting. As a class, discuss the following questions:

- What is the pope's role in the Church?
- Why would he imitate Jesus this way?
- Whose feet is Pope Francis washing?
- Why would the pope wash the feet of prisoners?

Wrap Up

A. Discuss how the pope is Christ's representative on Earth and called to imitate Christ in a special way. Then ask your students if *only* priests and religious are called to be like Christ. Of course the answer is no: we are all called to live as Christ did.

B. For homework, have students ask their parents to help them locate and bring in an image of a pope doing any of the following things:

- Caring for a sick person
- Visiting the imprisoned
- Feeding the hungry
- Helping the poor
- Offering advice or instruction
- Comforting someone

Next class, have students share the pictures they brought in for homework and explain what is happening in the pictures. When they are done, they should affix the pictures to a bulletin board or another display area.

HANDOUT A

Foot Washing

Directions: Look at the image and answer the questions below.

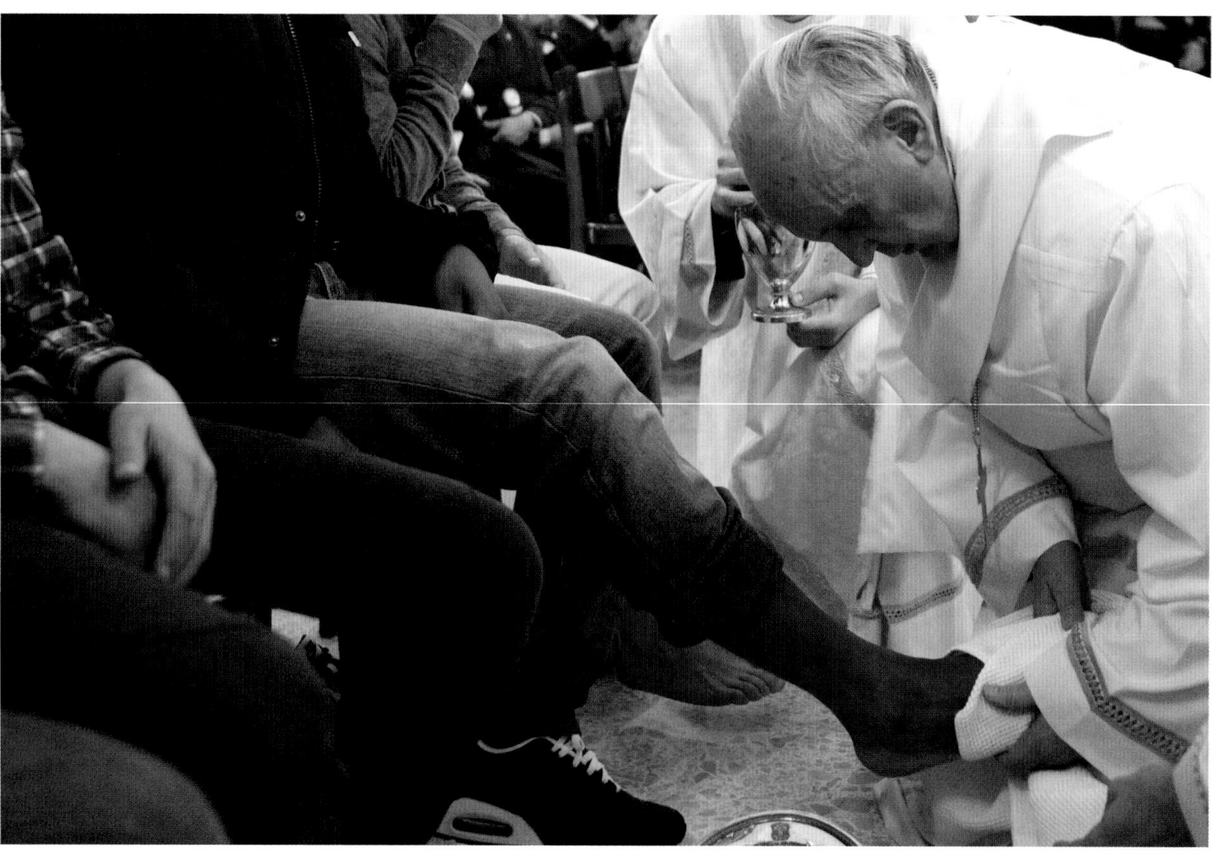

L'Osservatore Romano

1. Who is the man kneeling?

____

2. How does this image compare with the painting *Jesus Washing Peter's Feet* by Ford Madox Brown?

____

____

____

3. Choose one of the Bible verses below and write a short reflection in response.

____

____

____

____

____

____

The land will never lack for needy persons; that is why I command you: "Open your hand freely to your poor and to your needy kin in your land.

DEUTERONOMY 15:11

And the king will say to them in reply, "Amen, I say to you, whatever you did for one of these least brothers of mine, you did for me."

MATTHEW 25:40

In all things I have shown you that by working hard in this way we must help the weak and remember the words of the Lord Jesus, how he himself said, "It is more blessed to give than to receive."

ACTS 25:40

Answer Key

Sacred Art and Mercy: The Corporal and Spiritual Works of Mercy

1. Jesus Christ
2. Washing the feet of a man
3. St. Peter
4. The Apostles in the Upper Room at the Last Supper
5. Jesus washing the Apostles' feet on Holy Thursday
6. Accept reasoned answers.
7. Because he knows that Jesus is God the Son; only lowly servants were expected to wash feet.
8. Unless Peter is washed by Jesus, Peter will not go to heaven.
9. Jesus tells them that He has given them an example to follow. He models servant leadership, humility, unconditional love, and mercy. Accept additional reasoned answers.
10. These words remind us how Jesus cleanses our souls of sin. Students may make connections to the Sacraments of Baptism and Confession and the use of holy water and sacred chrism.

Handout A: Foot Washing

1. Pope Francis
2. Accept reasoned answers.
3. Accept reasoned answers.

Introduction to the Corporal and Spiritual Works of Mercy

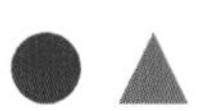

LESSON OVERVIEW

Learning Goals

- Works of Mercy are concrete ways in which we can live out our Faith.
- There are seven Corporal and seven Spiritual Works of Mercy.
- In Scripture, Christ not only instructs us on what the Works of Mercy are; He also provides examples in His ministry.
- As Catholics, we are called to be Christ in the world and build His Kingdom through our actions.

Connection to the Catechism

- CCC 1966-1970
- CCC 2447

Essential Questions

- What are the Corporal Works of Mercy?
- What are the Spiritual Works of Mercy?
- Why should we perform these works?

BIBLICAL TOUCHSTONES

Lord, you are good and forgiving, most merciful to all who call on you.

PSALMS 65:5

Do to others whatever you would have them do to you. This is the law and the prophets.

MATTHEW 7:12

● ES ▲ MS

Lesson Plan

Materials

- Handout A: The Corporal and Spiritual Works of Mercy

Warm-Up

A. Discuss with students that from what something is, we can tell what we **ought** to do. For example, say "A man is hungry. We **ought** to feed him." Or "A child is being bullied. We **ought** to stand up for him."

B. Call on a student to offer an original "is" statement, and then call on the next student to say the corresponding "ought" statement. Go around the room, alternating between "is" and "ought." If students struggle to come up with original statements, you could offer:

- A man is drowning, and you have a life preserver./You **ought** to throw it to him.
- A new student at your school is lonely./You **ought** to welcome him.
- A friend is struggling in math, and you are good at math./You **ought** to help him.
- A man is dying of thirst./You **ought** to give him water.
- An elderly person is walking onto a crowded bus./You **ought** to give her your seat.
- A friend is sick in the hospital./You **ought** to visit and cheer up your friend.

C. When it becomes your turn, make the statement: *You are created in God's image and likeness.* The class's response should be something to the effect of, *We **ought** to live like the Lord lives*, or *We should try to be like God.*

D. Ask students to volunteer some things they know about how Jesus lived. Accept reasoned answers that evidence Jesus' self-giving love and sacrifice on the Cross for our salvation. Lead students to the conclusion that in addition to suffering death, Jesus gave us many concrete examples of how to show love to one another. Encourage students to connect this discussion to Jesus' teachings: the greatest commandment, to love one another as He has loved us.

Activity

A. Have students complete **Handout A: The Corporal and Spiritual Works of Mercy** individually. They should then pair up and discuss their responses.

B. Call on a few students to share their responses with the class, providing correction as needed.

C. Ask students if any of the Works of Mercy are mysterious or hard to figure out? Aren't these all what we would want someone to do for us if we needed them to?

D. Write on the board the golden rule that Jesus gives us in Matthew 7:12 "Do to others whatever you would have them do to you. This is the law and the prophets."

E. Connect Jesus' teaching to the works of mercy, reminding students that the Church believes these works to be essential to the Christian life.

Wrap-Up

A. Ask students to define the word mercy on a slip of paper and put it into a shoe box or another container that you provide.

B. Then go around the room and have each student draw a slip from the shoe box or container with the students' definitions of mercy. Ask them to consider whether the definition fits with the one they had in mind. Call on a few students to read their definitions aloud and comment on whether they think the definition is correct and complete.

   Write on the board the definition of mercy provided in the glossary of the *Catechism of the Catholic Church*:

   > **MERCY:** *The loving kindness, compassion, or forbearance shown to one who offends.*

C. You might simplify this definition by explaining that mercy is love that keeps on loving even when it is rejected. When we sin, we reject God. But He never stops loving us. His mercy (or His love) is infinite. This kind of love is how we are called to love as Christians.

D. Explain that the Corporal and Spiritual Works of Mercy are charitable acts we can do for our neighbors. As Catholics, we are called to be Christ in the world and build His Kingdom through our actions. We love God above all, and we love one another as God has loved us.

HANDOUT B

The Corporal and Spiritual Works of Mercy

Directions: Read the works of mercy, looking up any words you don't know. Then write them out on the lines provided. Finally, answer the questions below.

The Corporal Works of Mercy are	Write the Corporal Works of Mercy
Feed the hungry.	__________
Give drink to the thirsty.	__________
Clothe the naked.	__________
Shelter the homeless.	__________
Visit the sick.	__________
Visit the imprisoned.	__________
Bury the dead.	__________

The Spiritual Works of Mercy are	Write the Spiritual Works of Mercy
Instruct the ignorant.	__________
Counsel the doubtful.	__________
Admonish the sinner.	__________
Bear wrongs patiently.	__________
Forgive offenses willingly.	__________
Comfort the afflicted.	__________
Pray for the living and the dead.	__________

Focus and Reflection Questions

1. What does *corporal* mean?
2. What does *spiritual* men?
3. What does *mercy* mean?
4. From where do we get these lists of works of mercy?

Reflection Questions:

5. Why do we need both Corporal and Spiritual Works of Mercy? Why wouldn't one or the other be enough?
6. Both the Corporal and the Spiritual Works of Mercy are essential to the Christian Life. Which do you think are more important, the Corporal Works of Mercy or the Spiritual Works of Mercy? Explain.

The works of mercy are not optional but are absolutely essential to living the Christian life of holiness and goodness

CCC 2447

Answer Key

Handout A: The Corporal and Spiritual Works of Mercy

1. Relating to the body
2. Relating to the soul
3. Mercy is love shown to someone who rejects that love.
4. From the teachings and example of Jesus Christ
5. Accept reasoned answers.
6. Accept reasoned answers, but guide students to the conclusion that because the spiritual works concern the state of a person's soul, they are more important. Performing spiritual works of mercy for another helps that person get to heaven.

Jesus Teaches Us How to Live the Works of Mercy

LESSON OVERVIEW

Learning Goals

- We must be open to God's saving love and keep His commandments if we want to have eternal life.
- He has commanded us to love one another as He has loved us.
- Works of Mercy are concrete ways in which we can love one another as Jesus loved us.
- Christ not only instructs us on what the acts of mercy are; He also provides examples in His ministry.
- As Catholics, we are called to be Christ in the world and build His Kingdom through our actions.

Connection to the Catechism

- CCC 1966-1970
- CCC 2447

Essential Question

- What examples of the Works of Mercy can we find in Jesus' life?

BIBLICAL TOUCHSTONES

The Lord is gracious and merciful, slow to anger and abounding in mercy.

PSALMS 145:8

Amen I say to you, whatever you did for one of these least brothers of mine, you did for me.

MATTHEW 25:40

● ES ▲ MS

Lesson Plan

Materials

- Holy Bible
- Handout A: Note-Taking Aid
- Handout C: Christ Our Teacher
- Appendix A: Saints of Mercy Cards
- Blank paper, colored pencils, markers
- Optional: Computers/ iPads

Background/Homework

Have students read Matthew 25:31-46 in their Bibles and come prepared to discuss it next class.

Warm-Up

A. Begin by explaining that Jesus' earthly ministry is full of examples of what it means to love one another. If we imitate Jesus, we are building His Kingdom in the world. This is what we are called to do as Christians. The Works of Mercy are essential to the Christian life.

B. Read Matthew 25:31-46 as students follow along in their Bibles. You may wish to read it aloud a second time, this time distributing **Handout A: Note-Taking Aid** for younger learners. Have students write down the Corporal Works of Mercy as you read.

C. Discuss how, since each human being has dignity as the image and likeness of God, when we help or do not help someone, we are helping or ignoring Christ. Note: *Students might wrongly object that "not helping" is not an action and therefore cannot be sinful. Have a brief discussion about acts of omission – if you choose not to help someone, you are in fact choosing to ignore him.*

Activity

A. Give each student one of the three cards on **Handout B: Christ Our Teacher** to complete independently.

B. Circulate around the room to offer assistance with looking up and interpreting passages.

C. Select students to share their responses with the class. Summarize the passage and identify the Work of Mercy.

Wrap-Up

A. Select and distribute appropriate cards from **Appendix A: Saints of Mercy Cards**. You could read their stories aloud or have students explore them in small groups.

B. Have students write on an index card in response to the reading:

- How this saint performed works of mercy
- Two or three ways in which they themselves can live out that act in their community

Extension Option

Prepare a Works of Mercy bulletin board. Read a few responses from the index cards from the last class. Then, as a class, identify a Corporal Work of Mercy students could complete that would engage the whole class or school (e.g., a food or clothing drive, illustrating place mats for a nursing home, or assembling kits for a homeless shelter).

Have students select one of the Scripture passages that they read (or another that illustrates the Work of Mercy the class has chosen) and illustrate it. Above the image, students should write the Scripture reference. Beneath the image, students should summarize the Scripture passage and identify the Work of Mercy. Alternatively, you may give students time with computers or iPads to find portrayals of their selected biblical passage in a work of fine art that could be displayed with their commentary – creating a gallery of sorts. When completed, the bulletin board will provide not only artworks generated or located by students but also information about the agency or people served and how students might participate in this event.

Send home the following note:

> *Dear parents,*
>
> *Your child has identified a corporal act of mercy to carry out in your community. Please help your child to accomplish this goal or another act of mercy and talk about the experience. Then help your child think of some other ways in which he or she might perform acts of mercy in your neighborhood and parish community.*

HANDOUT A

Note-Taking Aid

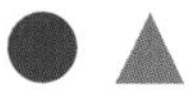

Directions: Listen as your teacher reads aloud from Matthew's Gospel. Write out the Corporal Works of Mercy on the lines below:

Focus and Reflection Questions

1. How would you describe Jesus' tone in this passage? (Tone means a speaker's attitude toward his subject.) Does it sound as if Jesus is teaching us something optional, or something very serious? How do you know?
2. At Holy Mass, we ask forgiveness for what we have done, as well as for what we have failed to do. Can we love God if we fail to do Works of Mercy for our neighbors?
3. What do you think Jesus means by "Amen I say to you, whatever you did for one of these least brothers of mine, you did for me" (Matthew 25:40)?
4. Have you ever performed any of the Works of Mercy that Jesus describes? Has anyone ever done them for you? Tell a story about that time in the space below.

____

____

____

____

____

But you, brothers, do not be remiss in doing good.

2 THESSALONIANS 3:13

Christ Our Teacher

Teacher Note: Differentiate the lesson by offering different versions to different students. Version 3 is more challenging than versions 1 and 2.

1

Directions

1. Look up the Bible passage and read it.
2. Write a 2-3 sentence summary of the passage.
3. Identify the Work of Mercy referenced in the passage.

Passages

A. Luke 18:35-43 ______________________________

B. Matthew 14:15-21 ______________________________

2

Directions

1. Look up the Bible passage and read it.
2. Write a 2-3 sentence summary of the passage.
3. Identify the Work of Mercy referenced in the passage.

Passages

A. Luke 10:29-37______________________________

B. Matthew 8:1-3 ______________________________

3

Directions

1. Look up the Bible passage and read it.
2. Write a 2-3 sentence summary of the passage.
3. Identify the Work of Mercy referenced in the passage.

Passages

A. Mark 5:2-15 ____________________________________

B. John 8:1-11 ____________________________________

4

Directions

1. Look up the Bible passage and read it.
2. Write a 2-3 sentence summary of the passage.
3. Identify the Work of Mercy referenced in the passage.

Passages

A. Luke 7:36-50 ____________________________________

B. Luke 23:33-43 ____________________________________

Answer Key

Handout B: Christ Our Teacher

Version 1

A. Luke 18: 35-43: Visit the sick. Jesus speaks with a blind beggar even though others ignore the man. Jesus heals the beggar of his blindness.

B. Matthew 14:15-21: Feed the hungry. Jesus had many people following him, and they are growing hungry. Jesus provides food for them in the miracle of the loaves and fishes.

Version 2

A. Luke 10: 29-37: Shelter the homeless; also, visit the sick, feed the hungry. In the parable of the good Samaritan, the Samaritan helps the man and brings him to an inn to care for him when others would not do so.

B. Matthew 8: 1-3: Visit the sick. Jesus was asked to heal a leper. Jesus did so when others in His society would not even consider touching someone with leprosy.

Version 3

A. Mark 5: 2-15: Comfort the afflicted; Visit the sick. Jesus visits the sick—in this case someone who is mentally ill and possessed by demons. Christ offers comfort to him and heals him of his affliction.

B. John 8: 1-11: Admonish sinners; Visit the imprisoned. A woman has broken a law and is condemned to death. Jesus forgives her and He tells her not to sin anymore.

Version 4

A. Luke 7:36-50: Forgive all injuries, instruct the ignorant. Jesus forgives the sins of a woman whom the Pharisees had condemned as a sinner. He explains that she shows love because she has experienced forgiveness.

B. Luke 23:33-43: Forgive all injuries, bear wrongs patiently, pray for the living and the dead. Jesus prays to the Father to forgive His executioners and forgives the sins of the criminal hanging next to him.

Mercy's Work of Showing God's Love

LESSON OVERVIEW

Learning Goals

- We are physical and spiritual beings; the Works of Mercy are both physical and spiritual.
- Exploring the Latin roots of corporal and spiritual can help us understand the Corporal and Spiritual Works of Mercy.
- The Spiritual Works of Mercy relieve universal needs.
- Although the Corporal and Spiritual Works of Mercy are both essential, the Spiritual Works are more important because they relieve needs directly related to our salvation.
- The Works of Mercy are based in Scripture.
- Jesus gives us a perfect model of what it means to love one another through the works of mercy.

Connection to the Catechism

- CCC 463
- CCC 1485
- CCC 2447

Essential Questions

- What is love?
- What can the Latin roots of corporal and spiritual teach us about the Works of Mercy?
- Which are more important: the Corporal Works of Mercy or the Spiritual Works of Mercy? Why?
- What can Scripture teach us about the Works of Mercy?

BIBLICAL TOUCHSTONES

Then the LORD God formed the man out of the dust of the ground and blew into his nostrils the breath of life, and the man became a living being.

GENESIS 2:7

So, too, it is written, "The first man, Adam, became a living being," the last Adam a life-giving spirit

1 CORINTHIANS 15:45

Lesson Plan

Materials

- Holy Bible
- Handout A: Mercy's Work of Showing God's Love
- Handout B: Latin Roots
- Handout C: He Breathed on Them
- Handout D: Mark 9:14-29 Reading Guide
- Handout E: Spiritual Works of Mercy in Scripture
- Large blank paper/poster board, markers

Background/Homework

A. Have students read **Handout A: Mercy's Work of Showing God's Love** and answer the focus and reflection questions.

B. Students should also reflect on a time when they were the recipient of a Spiritual Work of Mercy, and write a brief journal-style reflection on what happened.

Warm Up I

A. Have students stand up and tell them to listen actively to each thing you are about to say. For each, they should sit if what you say is a Corporal Work of Mercy and stand if it is a Spiritual Work of Mercy. Read the Corporal and Spiritual Works of Mercy in random order.

B. Now do a similar activity, asking students to sit if the phrase you say refers to something physical and to stand if it relates to something spiritual.

- The soul *(spiritual)*
- The body *(physical)*
- Tears *(physical)*
- Sorrow *(spiritual)*
- Laughter *(physical)*
- Joy *(spiritual)*
- Love *(This one should elicit discussion, as love is both physical and spiritual.)*
- The Sacraments *(both)*
- God *(both)*

C. Tie together the last three examples by reminding students that God is love, and that mercy is love that keeps loving even when it is rejected. Jesus was Incarnate of the Virgin Mary and became man. He dwelt among us, suffered and died for us, and entrusted the Sacraments to the Church because God loves us as both physical and spiritual beings. The Corporal and Spiritual Works of Mercy give us a way to love each other as God loves us.

Warm-up II

A. Ask if anyone knows what the word *derive* means. Tell students that we call words that *derive* from other languages *derivatives*. Have students complete **Handout B: Latin Roots** alone or in pairs.

B. Go over the derivatives and then have students share their original sentences using derivatives of *corpus* and *spiritus*.

C. Begin a discussion of *corpus*. Discuss the two meanings of the word *body* – a physical body and a body as in a group with members. Connect these two meanings of the word body to the Body of Christ. The Church is the Body of Christ; when we are baptized we become members of His Body. And we receive the Body of Christ in the Eucharist. These two Sacraments were born when blood and water flowed from the side of Christ after His Crucifixion.

D. Draw students' attention to the way the derivatives of *spiritus* don't have immediately obvious connections to "breath," e.g. "conspire," or "aspirations."

Activity

A. Together, read aloud John 20:19-23. Then have students complete **Handout C: He Breathed on Them**. Go over responses as a group, using the Answer Key as a guide.

B. Transition the discussion to the Spiritual Works of Mercy, and invite students to share their journal reflections, invite them to do so. If no students wish to share, ask if anyone has never been the recipient of a spiritual Work of Mercy. The goal is to help students understand that the feelings or states that the Spiritual Works of Mercy help (doubt, sorrow, ignorance, and so forth) are universals. Everyone experiences at least some of them at some point in their lives. We should go to Jesus in prayer seeking His comfort and relief of our doubt, our sorrow, and so forth. Christ continues His ministry in the Church, and the Sacraments are precious gifts that allow us to receive His love and grace here on Earth. And remember that He calls us to love one another as He has loved us. We are called to love and care for one another in this life through the Works of Mercy.

Wrap-Up

A. Have students turn to chapter 9 of the Gospel of Mark and follow along as you read aloud verses 14–29.

B. Have students complete **Handout D: Mark 9:14–29 Reading Guide**. As a large group, challenge students to find examples of Works of Mercy in this passage. How does Jesus:

- Counsel the doubtful? *He gives advice to all those who disbelieve, especially the boy's father. He tells him, "Everything is possible to one who has faith."*
- Bear wrongs patiently? *He remains with those who disbelieve, despite their failures.*
- Comfort the afflicted? *He releases the boy from the demon and gives comfort to his father.*
- Instruct the ignorant? *He explains to the disciples why they were unable to cast out the demon.*
- Accept additional reasoned answers.

Enrichment Options

A. Have students create a concept web linking the words *corpus* and *spiritus*. Encourage students to include words, phrases, names, Scripture verses, and other things they have learned in this lesson. Post completed webs around the room and give students time to view them all.

B. Have students complete **Handout E: Spiritual Works of Mercy in Scripture**. To differentiate instruction, consider the following variations:

- Put students in pairs and have each pair look up and respond to one Bible verse. Then jigsaw into new groups of eight and have students complete **Handout E** as they teach each other about their assigned verses.
- Put students in pairs or trios and have them complete all of **Handout E** together; then debrief as a large group.
- Have students complete **Handout E** individually.

Mercy's Work of Showing God's Love

Jesus tells us to love one another, saying "This is my commandment: love one another as I love you" (John 15:12). Far from the warm fuzzy feelings of the modern notion of love, Jesus tells us to love as He loved. The question is: How did Jesus love us? St. John the Evangelist explains, "In this is love: not that we have loved God, but that he loved us and sent his Son as expiation for our sins" (1 John 4:10). Further, Jesus says, "No one has greater love than this, to lay down one's life for one's friends" (John 15:13).

The greatest expression of love is self-sacrifice, giving oneself as a gift for the good of another. On the night before He died, Jesus gathered with His Apostles for their last meal together. He took bread, said the blessing, broke it, and gave it to them saying, "Take and eat; this is my body" (Matthew 26:26). Similarly, He took the cup of wine, gave thanks, and gave it to them saying, "Drink from it, all of you, for this is my blood of the covenant, which will be shed on behalf of many for the forgiveness of sins" (Matthew 16:27). And, the next day, Jesus sacrificed Himself on the Cross, fulfilling His words by His actions. Christ loved us by giving Himself freely and completely to us in an act of mercy.

Christ Carrying the Cross, El Greco

The Commandment to love can feel difficult, especially when Jesus teaches us to love even our enemies. Today many people wrongly think of love as a "feeling." We mistakenly say that love is something we can fall in and out of; we mistake love for an emotion that happens to us rather than something we freely choose to do. But if love were a feeling, why would a mother or father stay up all night with a sick baby even while feeling exhausted? If love were a feeling, why would a mother or father work two jobs to support the family when relaxing in the evenings and on weekends would feel so much better? If love were a feeling, why would Jesus have endured the suffering of the Cross?

The truth is that all these ways of loving are possible because love is not a feeling but a choice, an action. We live in a culture that tells us to put feelings above all else, that we can "fall out of love," and so forth, but the truth is that we do not have to live as slaves to our feelings. When we chose self-giving love even when it doesn't "feel good" to do so, just as spouses, parents, family, and friends do, we share in the Lord's self-giving love. "God himself is an eternal exchange of love, Father, Son and Holy Spirit, and he has destined us to share in that exchange" (CCC 221). It would not make sense for Jesus to command us to simply and passively "feel" something. Rather, He commands us to offer ourselves for the good of another, just as He Himself did for humanity. This highest form of freely chosen, self-giving love is called *agape*. When the Bible talks of how God loved the world, the verb used is *agape*.

To love as Christ loves is to imitate Him by embracing His mercy and offering it to one another in sacrifice. This is our calling, our universal vocation of holiness. In response to Christ's command to be perfect as the Father is perfect, the council fathers of Vatican II wrote in *Lumen Gentium*, "In order to reach this perfection, the faithful should use the strength dealt out to them by Christ's gift, so that ... doing the will of the Father in everything, they may wholeheartedly devote themselves to the glory of God and to the service of their neighbor." Because God loved us first and poured out His mercy upon us, we are able to serve one another, in love and mercy, encompassed in the petition of the Lord's Prayer: "forgive us our trespasses, as we forgive those who trespass against us."

By the grace of God, may we be strengthened to know His love, accept His mercy, and humbly serve our brothers and sisters in the spirit of that very same love and mercy of God!

Focus and Reflection Questions

1. Jesus teaches us not merely to love one another; He teaches us to love in a very special way. What is that way?
2. How do you know that love is not a feeling but a choice?
3. What is *agape*?
4. What do you think is the most challenging part of Jesus' commandment to love one another as He has loved us? What can you do today in order to answer this call?

Journal Reflection: Read over the Spiritual Works of Mercy and reflect on each one. Have you ever been ignorant of something? What did you need to know? Have you ever been doubtful? Sorrowful? And so forth. Write a journal-style reflection in which you explain what happened, who helped you, and what the result was.

HANDOUT B

Latin Roots

Directions: Read about the meanings of the words *corporal* and *spiritual*. Read about each derivative, and underline the letters from the Latin root in each one. The first has been done for you.

Corporal	Spiritual
Corporal means relating to a **body**. The word *body* can refer to a human body or to a group of members of a body. *Corporal* comes from the Latin word *corpus*, which means **body**.	*Spiritual* means relating to the soul. *Spiritual* comes from the Latin word *spiritus*, which means **breath**.
Derivatives	**Derivatives**
A dead human **body** is called a *corpse* (with "corp" underlined). *Corporal* punishment means a punishment that affects a person's **body**, such as spanking. A *corps*, like the Marine *Corps*, is a **body** of soldiers. In military ranks, a *corporal* is in charge of a **body** of soldiers. A *corporation* is a group of people making up the **body** of a business or club. We call Christ's **Body** on a Crucifix the *Corpus*. *Corpus Christi* means the **Body** of Christ.	*Respiration* (with "spir" underlined) means **breathing**. A medical device that **breathes** for a patient is called a *respirator*. To *conspire* means to work or plan together. *Aspirations* are your goals and dreams. Your enthusiasm for your school can be called your school *spirit*. The third Divine Person of the Trinity is the Holy *Spirit*.

Corporal	Spiritual
Corporal means relating to a **body**. The word *body* can refer to a human body or to a group of members of a body. *Corporal* comes from the Latin word *corpus*, which means **body**.	*Spiritual* means relating to the soul. *Spiritual* comes from the Latin word *spiritus*, which means **breath**.
Write a sentence using at least one derivative of *corpus*. ____________________ ____________________ ____________________ ____________________ ____________________	Write a sentence using at least one derivative of *spiritus*. ____________________ ____________________ ____________________ ____________________ ____________________

Respiration means **breathing**. To *aspirate* means to **breathe** out. These derivatives of *spiritus* have clear connections to the word *breath*. But what about the words below?

1. A medical device that doctors use to check a person's lungs is called a *spirometer*.

   What is the connection to breath?

   ____

   ____

2. *Aspirations* are your goals and dreams.

   What is the connection to breath?

   ____

   ____

3. Your enthusiasm for your school can be called your school *spirit*.

   What is the connection to breath?

   ____

   ____

Reflection Question: The third Divine Person of the Trinity is the Holy *Spirit*.

What is the connection to breath? Write a paragraph in response to this question below:

____

____

____

____

____

____

____

Say the Sign of the Cross in Latin!
Do you see the Latin words for *Holy Spirit*?

SIGNUM CRUCIS

In nomine Patris, et Filii, et Spiritus Sancti. Amen.

HANDOUT C

He Breathed On Them

▲ ■

Directions: Answer the questions below after reading John 20:19-23.

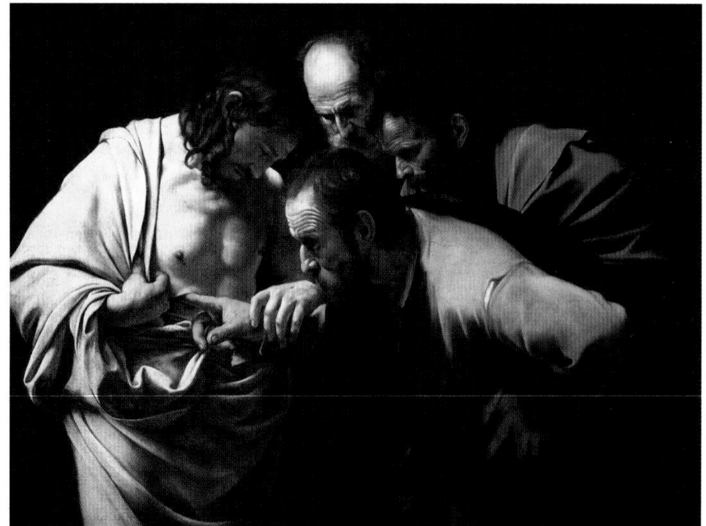

The Incredulity of Saint Thomas, Caravaggio

1. Where did the conversation between Jesus and His disciples take place?
2. When did it take place?
3. Why did Jesus show them His hands and His side?
4. What happens in John 20:22?
5. Why do you think this Gospel is considered one of the scriptural bases for the sacrament of Confession?
6. Read Genesis 2:7. How does the sacred author describe God's forming the first man?
7. Read 1 Corinthians 15:45. Whom is St. Paul calling "the last Adam"?
8. How did Jesus breathe life into the disciples?
9. How does He breathe life into the Church?
10. How does He breathe life into **you**?

Reflection Question: Which Works of Mercy are more important, the Corporal or Spiritual?

> Then the LORD God formed the man out of the dust of the ground and blew into his nostrils the breath of life, and the man became a living being.
>
> GENESIS 2:7

> So, too, it is written, "The first man, Adam, became a living being," the last Adam a life-giving spirit.
>
> 1 CORINTHIANS 15:45

HANDOUT D

Mark 9:14-29 Reading Guide

Directions: Read Mark 9:14-29. Then read it through once more according to the directions below.

1. Read verses 14-18. What does the man in the crowd tell Jesus?

   ____

2. How does Jesus respond in verses 19-23?

   ____

3. What does the boy's father cry out in line 24? Does he seem to contradict himself? How should we understand what he is asking Jesus to do?

Icon, Jesus casting out demons

4. Is this request something only the boy's father can ask for? Can we all ask God to strengthen our faith? Explain.

____

____

____

5. How many Works of Mercy can you find Jesus performing in this story?

____

____

____

HANDOUT E

Spiritual Works of Mercy in Scripture

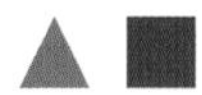

Directions: Look up the following Bible verses and explain in one or two sentences the connection(s) to the Spiritual Works of Mercy.

Galatians 6:1

____

____

Colossians 3:16

____

____

Isaiah 66:13

____

____

Galatians 6:2

____

____

Colossians 3:12-13

____

____

Ephesians 6:18

____

____

Answer Key

Handout A: Mercy's Work of Showing God's Love

1. As He has loved us.
2. We know that love is a choice and not just a feeling because it would not make sense for Jesus to command us to passively experience a feeling. But the command to love makes sense because we freely choose to love.
3. *Agape* is self-sacrificial love for the good of another. Students should recognize that *agape* is an act of will.
4. Accept reasoned answers.

Handout B: Latin Roots

1. Our lungs are the organs that allow us to breathe.
2. The things we aspire to do could be considered breaths of air into our lives. Accept additional reasoned answers.
3. The energy or spirit of a school or team gives it life and energy. Accept additional reasoned answers.
4. Responses should touch on the way the Holy Spirit is the giver of life. He proceeds from the Father and the Son and breathes life into the Church and into all Christians.

Handout C: He Breathed on Them

1. In the Upper Room.
2. After Jesus' Resurrection.
3. To help them believe that He was who He said He was: to show them the wounds on His hands from His Crucifixion, as well as His side, from which blood and water poured out when it was pierced by a Roman solider.
4. Jesus breathes on them and tells them to receive the Holy Spirit.
5. The Apostles were the first priests. Jesus gives the first priests the sacred power to forgive sins in His Name.
6. Blowing into his nostrils.
7. Jesus Christ.

8. Accept reasoned answers. Encourage students to make connections to the gifts of the Holy Spirit.
9. Through all of the Sacraments, especially the Eucharist; the gifts of the Holy Spirit. Accept additional reasoned answers.
10. Accept reasoned answers. Encourage students to make connections to Jesus' commands to love God and neighbor and to perform the Corporal and Spiritual works of Mercy.

Reflection Question: Although both are essential to the Christian life, the Spiritual Works of Mercy are more important. They are more important because they address needs that are related to the ultimate end for which we are created: beatitude, or an eternity in heaven with God. In other words, we perform the Spiritual Works of Mercy for our neighbors to help them get to heaven.

Handout D: Mark 9:14-29 Reading Guide

1. His son is afflicted by a demon.
2. He admonishes the crowd for their lack of faith and tells them to bring Him the boy.
3. "I do believe, help my unbelief." Accept reasoned answers. Students should recognize that the boys father believes, but with reservations. In other words, he doubts. He has a measure of faith, but he begs the Lord to help him trust fully.
4. The boy's father is, in essence, praying for the Lord to strengthen his faith. We can all offer this type of prayer.
5. Accept reasoned answers along the lines of the suggestions given in the lesson plan.

Handout E: Works of Mercy in Scripture

Galatians 6:1: ""Brothers, even if a person is caught in some transgression, you who are spiritual should correct that one in a gentle spirit." We are called to admonish sinners.

Colossians 3:16: "Let the word of Christ dwell in you richly, as in all wisdom you teach and admonish one another." We should instruct people in the Faith, which includes admonishing sinners, and help them become wise.

Isaiah 66:13: "As a mother comforts her child, so I will comfort you." We should comfort those who are suffering.

Galatians 6:2: "Bear one another's burdens, and so you will fulfill the law of Christ." This verse relates to both corporal and spiritual burdens, and thus both the Corporal and Spiritual Works of Mercy. Hunger is a burden; ignorance is a burden, and so forth.

Colossians 3:12-13: “Put on then, as God’s chosen ones, holy and beloved, heartfelt compassion, kindness, humility, gentleness, and patience, bearing with one another and forgiving one another, if one has a grievance against another; as the Lord has forgiven you, so must you also do.” We are called to bear wrongs patiently, and forgive our neighbors.

Ephesians 6:18: “With all prayer and supplication, pray at every opportunity in the Spirit. To that end, be watchful with all perseverance and supplication for all the holy ones.” “All” includes the living and the dead.

Saints of Mercy

LESSON OVERVIEW

Learning Goals

- At the heart of God's Divine Mercy is His never-ending love for us.
- The central teaching of the Divine Mercy message delivered to St. Faustina is to ask God for His mercy, to be merciful toward others, and to trust completely in Jesus.
- The saints give us many examples of living God's mercy in our daily lives.

Connection to the Catechism

- CCC 1473
- CCC 1846-1848
- CCC 2447

Essential Questions

- What is the central teaching of Divine Mercy?
- What can we learn from the saints about living God's mercy?

BIBLICAL TOUCHSTONES

The Lord said: "[T]his people draws near with words only and honors me with their lips alone, though their hearts are far from me..."

ISAIAH 29:13

Blessed are the merciful, for they will be shown mercy.

MATTHEW 5:7

The Divine Mercy Image

BY EUGENIUSZ KAZIMIROWSKI (1934)

DIGITAL IMAGES AVAILABLE AT
WWW.SOPHIAINSTITUTEFORTEACHERS.ORG

Sacred Art and Mercy
The Divine Mercy Image

The Divine Mercy Image, *Eugeniusz Kazimirowski, 1934*

Directions: Take some time to quietly view and reflect on the art. Let yourself be inspired in any way that happens naturally. Then think about the questions below, and discuss them with your classmates.

Conversation Questions

1. What is the first word or phrase that comes to your mind when you first look at this image?
2. What do the two different color beams of light in the Divine Mercy image represent?
3. How does this image communicate the mercy of God?
4. How would you define mercy based on this image?
5. For each beam of light, describe one way it has been communicated in Salvation History.
6. Read the following Scriptures:
    - The Lord said: "Since this people draws near with words only and honors me with their lips alone, though their hearts are far from me..." ISAIAH 29:13
    - "Blessed are the merciful, for they will be shown mercy." MATTHEW 5:7

    In what ways are these Scriptures represented by the Divine Mercy image and the story of how it came to be?
7. In her diary, St. Faustina recorded these words of Jesus in reference to the Divine Mercy Image: "Not in the beauty of the color, nor of the brush lies the greatness of this image, but in My grace" (313). There are many different versions of the Divine Mercy image. What does Jesus teach about these images and what is truly important?

Lesson Plan

Materials

- Sacred Art and Mercy: The Divine Mercy Image
- Handout A: Saints of Mercy
- Appendix A: Saints of Mercy Cards

Background/Homework

Have students read the biographies of St. Faustina and Pope St. John Paul II from their Saint Cards. Have students come to class prepared to explain one way each of these saints emphasized the Divine Mercy during his or her lifetime.

Warm-Up I

Have students turn to a neighbor and share one way in which St. Faustina and Pope St. John Paul II emphasized the Divine Mercy during their lifetimes.

Warm-Up II

A. Project the image of the Divine Mercy image by Eugeniusz Kazimirowski from **Sacred Art and Mercy: The Divine Mercy Image**. Give students several minutes to quietly view the art before you say or ask anything. Allow them to come up and stand closer to the image to examine details.

B. Ask students what this is an image of. Explain that this is the Divine Mercy image. There are many different versions of this painting, but this particular version, is the original image that St. Faustina asked Eugeniusz Kazimirowsk to paint.

C. Project the Divine Mercy on the board. Give students some time to quietly view the art again before you say or ask anything.

D. Put students in small groups and give each group a laminated copy of **Sacred Art and Mercy: The Divine Mercy Image**. Have them discuss the questions on the back of the handout with each other. During this time, focus on keeping students intent on the artwork and the discussion questions, letting their conversations go in unexpected ways.

E. Call on groups in turn to share their answers and discuss each of the questions.

Activity

A. Explain to your students that at the heart of God's Divine Mercy is His never-ending love for us. Despite our sinfulness and unfaithfulness, God's love for us never dies. God always remains faithful. We, however, must receive God's love and mercy. This central teaching of the Divine Mercy message delivered to St. Faustina by Jesus is as simple as ABC:

- **A**sk God for His mercy.
- **B**e merciful toward others.
- **C**ompletely trust in Jesus.

We ask for God's mercy through prayer and frequent reception of the Sacrament of Reconciliation and the Eucharist. After we have received God's mercy, we in turn spread God's love and mercy to others. The graces we receive from God require our complete trust in Jesus in order to bear fruit in our lives.

B. Project on the board and have a student stand and read aloud the following statement of Jesus as recorded by St. Faustina in her diary:

> "I demand from you deeds of mercy which are to arise out of love for me. You are to show mercy to your neighbors always and everywhere. You must not shrink from this or try to excuse yourself from it." (*Diary*, 742)

C. Ask your students what Jesus demands of us when we receive His love. *Deeds or acts of mercy toward others.*

D. Explain that throughout the centuries, there have been many holy people who have heeded God's call to receive mercy, to be merciful, and to trust in Jesus. These people are the saints in heaven, who have run the race and won the prize before us, by emptying themselves and being filled instead with God's love and mercy. As we've learned, the Church prescribes the Corporal and Spiritual Works of Mercy for us to follow in order to bring God's mercy to others.

E. Ask your students to name the Corporal and Spiritual Works of Mercy and list them on the board. *The Corporal Works of Mercy are: visit the imprisoned, clothe the naked, bury the dead, visit the sick, shelter the homeless, feed the hungry, and give drink to the thirsty. The Spiritual Works of Mercy are: forgive offenses willingly, instruct the ignorant, bear wrongs patiently, comfort the afflicted, pray for the living and the dead, counsel the doubtful, and admonish the sinner.*

F. The saints put into action the Works of Mercy and gave us a model to follow.

G. Arrange students into seven groups. Distribute to each group two different Saint Cards from **Appendix A: Saints of Mercy Cards**.

H. Also distribute a copy of **Handout A: Saints of Mercy** to each student. Have each group read their Saint Cards and complete **Handout A**. Circulate the room and assist as needed.

I. Although every saint provides an example of several Works of Mercy, you may wish to give each student a Saint Card from each of the following groups:

Corporal Works of Mercy

St. Peter Nalasco
St. Martin of Tours
St. Catherine of Siena
St. Vincent de Paul
Bl. Pier Giorgio
St. Maximilian Kolbe
St. Peter Claver
Bl. Miguel Pro
Servant of God Dorothy Day

Spiritual Works of Mercy

Mary, Mother of Mercy
St. Faustina
St. Margaret Mary Alacoque
St. Maria Goretti
St. Francis Xavier
St. Bernadette
St. Ignatius
Pope St. John Paul II
St. Teresa of Avila
St. Therese of Lisieux
St. Jean-Marie Vianney

Wrap-Up

A. Have each group choose one of the saints they studied, stand, and briefly explain how the saint lived out a specific Work of Mercy during his or her life.

B. End by praying together a Divine Mercy Chaplet. After the chaplet, pray a mini litany of saints, imploring the prayers of the saints studied in this lesson, using the following format:

Leader: Saint ______________________,

All: Pray for us.

HANDOUT B

Examples of Forgiveness and Healing from the Saints

Directions: Read the Saint Cards given to you and complete the chart.

Saint	Which Work of Mercy did this saint live out in a special way and how?	What example did this saint give for your own call to holiness?

Respond to the following prompt in a well-written paragraph of at least five to seven sentences:

Choose one of the saints you studied and imagine that he or she lived in your community today. What would that saint be doing? How would he or she be living out Works of Mercy? How would the community respond to the saint? What would be challenging about the example he or she set in your community?

APPENDIX A

Saints of Mercy Cards

Saints included in this section are:

- St. Peter Nalasco
- St. Martin of Tours
- St. Catherine of Sienna
- St. Vincent de Paul
- Bl. Pier Giorgio Frassati
- St. Maximilian Kolbe
- St. Peter Claver
- St. Faustina
- St. Margaret Mary Alacoque
- St. Maria Goretti
- St. Francis Xavier
- St. Bernadette
- Servant of God Dorothy Day
- St. Therese of Lisieux
- St. Jean-Marie Vianney
- St. Ignatius of Loyola
- Mary, Mother of Mercy
- Pope St. John Paul II
- St. Teresa of Avila
- Bl. Miguel Pro

In many cases, specific Works of Mercy are mentioned in a saint's card. However, many additional possibilities for connections between saints' lives and the Works of Mercy are possible. For example, St. Maximilian Kolbe not only fed the hungry as noted on his card; he also sheltered the homeless, counseled the doubtful, and comforted the afflicted.

The *Saints of Mercy* lesson in this guide contains a graphic organizer to help students understand how each saint lived out the Corporal and Spiritual Works of Mercy. You may also wish to use the following chart to brainstorm together how the saints featured in this book and others lived out each work. Challenge students to recall saints they have studied in the past, and to think "outside the box" in order to see how the Works of Mercy fit together as a coherent whole.

Works of Mercy and the Saints Chart

Corporal Works of Mercy	Saints in this Guide	Other Saints You've Studied
Feed the hungry		
Give drink to the thirsty		
Clothe the naked		
Shelter the homeless		
Visit the sick		
Visit the imprisoned		
Bury the dead		

The Spiritual Works of Mercy	Saints in this Guide	Other Saints You've Studied
Admonish the sinner		
Instruct the ignorant		
Counsel the doubtful		
Comfort the sorrowful		
Bear wrongs patiently		
Forgive all injuries		
Pray for the living and the dead		

Saint Cards

St. Margaret Mary Alacoque

1647-1690

Feast Day:
October 16

Margaret was born to a poor family in the Burgundy region of France. She developed a special devotion to the Blessed Sacrament, especially while she suffered a long illness. She was so sick that she could not get out of bed for years. One day she promised the Blessed Virgin Mary that she would enter religious life if she could be cured. Immediately, her health was restored. In thanks, Margaret took Mary as part of her first name. Margaret entered the convent at the age of 23.

Margaret reported that Jesus several times, and revealed to her devotions to His Sacred Heart. He said to her, "*My divine Heart is so inflamed with love for mankind ... that it can no longer contain within itself the flames of its burning charity and must spread them abroad by your means.*" Sister Margaret Mary described Jesus' heart as burning and encased by a crown of thorns. The flames were a sign of Jesus' love for humanity, and the crown of thorns was a symbol of our rejection of Him. Jesus also told Margaret that He wants people to receive the Eucharist on the first Friday of each month, spend an hour in Eucharistic adoration on Thursdays, and celebrate the Feast of the Sacred Heart.

At first, only Margaret's superior believed that Margaret had really seen and heard Jesus. But Margaret persisted, and eventually she was able to begin celebration of the Feast of the Sacred Heart in her convent. Later in a chapel was built nearby in honor of the Sacred Heart. Margaret died two years later. Her last words were, "I need nothing but God, and to lose myself in the heart of Jesus." Pope Pius IX officially added the Feast of the Sacred Heart to the Church calendar in 1856.

St. Bernadette

1844–1879

Feast Day:
April 16

St. Bernadette was the oldest of nine children born to a poor family in Lourdes, France. Bernadette was a sickly child and suffered many ailments throughout her life. When she was 14, Bernadette was collecting firewood when she heard the sound of rushing wind. When she looked around, she saw a rose floating in a grotto (a small cave). Then she saw a beautiful woman dressed in white with a blue sash. The woman asked Bernadette to come to the grotto every day for the next two weeks. Bernadette's parents did not believe her when she told them what she had seen. Many townspeople accused Bernadette of making the whole thing up

In all, Bernadette saw the apparition (or supernatural vision) 18 times. The woman instructed Bernadette to pray for sinners, do penance, and to have a chapel built on the spot of the visions. The woman also led Bernadette to discover a spring of water that had not been there before. Bernadette decided to ask the woman who she was. The woman replied "*Je suis L'Immaculate Conception*," French for "I am the Immaculate Conception." Immaculate Conception is a title of the Blessed Virgin Mary.

When she was old enough, Bernadette became a nun. She struggled with numerous illnesses. But in faithfulness to Jesus' command to beard wrongs patiently, as she did when she was a child, Bernadette offered all of her sufferings as penance for the sins of others. She died when she was 35. St. Bernadette was canonized by Pope Pius XI on December 8, 1933, the Solemnity of the Immaculate Conception. To this day, water still flows from the miraculous spring at Lourdes. Every year, 5 million people come from all over the world to drink and bathe in its healing waters.

St. Catherine of Siena

1347-1380

Feast Day:
April 29

Catherine was born in Siena, Italy, the second youngest of 25 children. From her youth, Catherine joyfully dedicated herself to prayer and devotion.

At the age of 18, Catherine began living in constant prayer as a hermit. During this time she attracted many followers who wanted to imitate her way of life. Catherine was granted a vision in which she was spiritually "married" to Jesus. He placed a ring on her finger that was only visible to her and told her that her faith could overcome all temptations.

After three years in seclusion, Catherine and her followers began to minister to the poor, especially those suffering from the Bubonic Plague, which took millions of lives in Europe at this time. The disease was so terrible that healthy people would not care for or even touch the victims, leaving the dead unburied in homes and in the streets out of fear that they too would become sick. Answering Jesus' command to bury the dead, Catherine would tend to the needs of the Plague victims, prepare them for death, and see that they were buried, often burying them herself.

Catherine wrote many letters to royalty, nobles, religious, and even the pope. Through her letters, Catherine gained a reputation for wisdom, holiness, and ability to settle disputes. Catherine played an important role during a turbulent time in Church history with multiple men claiming to be pope. Catherine's devotion to the pope of Rome never wavered. She received many visions, and was even given stigmata, or the wounds of Christ.

In 1380, Catherine died of a stroke at the age of 33. She was canonized in 1461 by Pope Pius II, and given the title Doctor of the Church in 1970 by Pope Paul VI. This is a special title that means her writings are especially useful to Christians.

St. Peter Claver

1581 –1654

Feast Day:
September 9

St. Peter Claver was born to a wealthy Catholic family near Barcelona, Spain. He entered the Society of Jesus, or the Jesuits, at the age of 20, and he resolved to spend his life serving others in the colonies of New Spain in the Americas.

Claver arrived in Cartagena, in modern day Columbia, in 1610. There, he was moved by the plight of the African slaves from West Africa. Thousands of slaves were brought into Cartagena each year, even though two popes had prohibited the slave trade by papal decree.

Once Fr. Claver was ordained, he undertook his mission to the slaves with fervor. He would board the slave ships as soon as they docked and begin ministering to those who had survived the journey. Conditions aboard the ships were dismal. The holds were crowded, dirty, smelly, and disease-infested.

After the enslaved people had been moved to holding pens, Fr. Claver would bring them medicine, food and drink, and affirm their human dignity. Peter would also catechize the slaves using pictures and interpreters. Peter is said to have baptized over 300,000 enslaved people. Fr. Claver's mission fulfilled Jesus' call to give drink to the thirsty, not only by satisfying their actual thirst, but by satisfying their thirst for God and dignity. Fr. Claver spent the final four years of his life too sick to leave his room, and he died in 1654. Pope Leo XIII canonized St. Peter Claver in 1888 and declared him the patron Saint of missionary work among African peoples.

Servant of God Dorothy Day

1897–1980

Dorothy Day was born in New York, and came of age during a time when ideas about socialism and communism were spreading to the U.S. from Europe. Day become involved in socialist movements. After a series of failed relationships, she gave birth to a daughter.

Motherhood changed Day. She decided to have her daughter baptized in the Catholic Church. She went to Mass, read religious books, and became close with a Catholic nun. Her relationship with the "Church of the poor" grew. She was baptized at age 30.

Wishing to serve the poor and outcast, Dorothy and a friend founded the Catholic Worker movement in 1933. This group focused on living justly and serving the needs of others. She described the group's mission as: "Our rule is the Works of Mercy… It is the way of sacrifice, worship, a sense of reverence." She published *The Catholic Worker* newspaper to speak out against unjust working conditions, advocate peace, and spread Church teachings about social justice. This newspaper is still in circulation today.

Many viewed Day as a radical. But in truth, she lived out Christ's command to comfort the afflicted through her commitment to Catholic teaching, active concern for the poor, and work for peace and justice.

It had been love of neighbor that first drew her to the ideas of socialism. But Day came to see that love and violence were incompatible. She wrote in 1951 that love of neighbor could never justify the forced labor, torture, and murder of millions that went on in China and the Soviet Union. Like many saints who lived their early lives in sin, Day was converted to Christ by the grace of God and accomplished great works of love and mercy. She is a Servant of God, the first step in the journey towards sainthood.

St. Faustina

1905-1938

Feast Day:
October 5

Helena Kowalska was born in Poland. When she was 7, she went to Eucharistic Adoration. There she first felt called to be a nun. She wanted to enter a convent when she finished school but her parents would not allow it. So instead Helena worked to support herself and help her parents take care of her 9 siblings.

When Helena was 19, she saw a vision of Jesus suffering. She went into a nearby church to pray and saw Jesus again; He told her to go to Warsaw. She packed and left for Warsaw the next morning. There she entered a convent, and took the name Faustina, which means "blessed one." Her tasks were gardening and cooking for the other sisters.

When she was 25, Jesus appeared to Sr. Faustina with light streaming out of His heart. He told her to have a painting made of what she saw, with the words "Jesus, I trust in you." Jesus told Sr. Faustina that He wanted the Sunday after Easter to be devoted to His mercy. Sr. Faustina told all this to Fr. Sopocko, her spiritual director. Fr. Sopocko helped Sr. Faustina; he asked a friend to paint Faustina's vision.

With the Archbishop's permission, Fr. Sopocko set the painting in a church and offered Mass devoted to Divine Mercy on the Sunday after Easter. Jesus visited Sr. Faustina to teach her a prayer called the Divine Mercy Chaplet. He asked her to spread the news of His mercy for everyone. She wrote down what Jesus said to her, so we can read His words in her diaries. Sr. Faustina grew very sick, and she was sent to a convent near her family's home. Jesus visited her there many times until she died at the age of 33.

Pope St. John Paul II kept a special devotion to St. Faustina and the Divine Mercy. He made the Sunday after Easter an official feast of the Church – Divine Mercy Sunday.

St. Pier Giorgio Frassati

1901-1925

Feast Day:
July 4

Pier was born to a wealthy family in Turin, Italy. He went to Mass, received Communion daily, and spent many nights in Eucharistic adoration. He loved to go hiking and mountain climbing trips with his friends, and would lead them in song and prayer throughout the day.

Pier joined the St. Vincent de Paul Society when he was 17. He took care of sick people, orphans, and disabled veterans returning from World War I. He wanted to be a mining engineer so that he could serve Christ among the miners. He spent his free time in college helping the poor.

When he was 18, he joined a student organization for social reform. He helped in starting a newspaper on the conditions, rights, and duties of workers. He spent summer vacations in Turin to serve the poor, heeding Christ's call to shelter the homeless by giving them everything he had and doing all he could to help them.

When he was 20, he helped to organize the first convention of Pax Romana, an association for uniting Catholic students from around the world to work together for peace.

Just before he was to graduate, he fell sick with polio. He wrote a note to a friend asking that his medicine be given to a poor man who needed it. He died at age 24. At his funeral, his parents were amazed to see huge crowds of the poor people and learn that their son had helped them all.

St. Maria Goretti

1890-1902

Feast Day:
July 6

Maria Goretti was born and lived in Italy. Her parents were so poor that they had to live in a house with another family and work on other people's farms. The family prayed together and loved each other deeply. Maria's father died when she was nine. Her mother took her father's place working on the farm, and Maria took her mother's place working in the home and caring for her youngest sister.

When Maria was 11, one of the sons of the other family, Alessando, tried to rape Maria. Maria, even as she feared for her own life, tried to tell Alessandro he was committing a mortal sin. She tried to warn him crying out as she struggled, "It is a sin. You would go to hell for it!" Alessandro then stabbed Maria. Maria was found by her mother and rushed to the hospital, but she was too deeply injured for the doctors to heal her.

As she was dying, Maria spoke with her mother. Maria said that that she forgave Alessandro and wanted him to be in Heaven with her. Then she died. Alessandro was not sorry for what he did until Maria appeared to him in a dream while he was in prison for her murder. She gave him lilies that felt hot in his hands. The next morning Alessandro repented and confessed his sin. He spent almost 30 years in prison for his crime. When he was released from prison, he went immediately to Maria's mother and begged her forgiveness, and she forgave him. Alessandro lived at a Capuchin monastery for the rest of his life, praying often for Maria's intercession as his "protector."

Like Jesus, Maria was an innocent person who died for the sins of her attacker. She beautifully responded to Jesus' call to forgive. She was canonized forty-eight years after her death by Pope Pius XII. Her mother, some of her siblings, and Alessandro were there.

St. Ignatius

1491-1556

Feast Day:
July 31

Ignatius was the youngest of thirteen children of a wealthy Spanish family. When he was 30, a cannonball injured his legs. He was carried to the hospital in Loyola. During his recovery, Ignatius read books about the life of Jesus. He read about prayer, and the lives of the Saints. He was very inspired by the simplicity of the life of St. Francis of Assisi.

When Ignatius recovered, he spent time in a monastery devoted to prayer. He left his sword and armor in a chapel dedicated to Mary. He gave all his clothes to the poor and wore a sack-cloth robe.

While a university student in Paris, Ignatius and six other students founded the Society of Jesus, or the Jesuit religious order. These seven men took vows of poverty, chastity, and obedience to the pope, and hoped to go evangelize the Holy Land. Ignatius and his companions were ordained priests. Ignatius wrote a Rule of life for his community to live by, and went to Rome to offer the services of the Society of Jesus to the Pope. The Pope welcomed them and wanted to send them out as missionaries. Ignatius's companions were sent to around the world to Portugal, India, Japan, Ireland, Germany and many other places to evangelize. Ignatius remained in Rome and directed all these men by writing letters to them. The missionaries founded schools, colleges, seminaries, and gathered more men into their order.

Inspired by his earlier readings about Jesus and prayer, Ignatius wrote the Spiritual Exercises. These exercises help people to pray. In keeping with the Spiritual Work of Mercy to admonish sinners, Ignatius's exercises encouraged people to examine their consciences and ask God to strengthen them to avoid sin. The missionaries had founded 100 religious houses, and the order had 1,000 members when Ignatius died.

Pope St. John Paul II

1920–2005

Feast Day: October 22

Karol Wojtyla was born in Poland, the youngest of three children. When he was a young man, the German Nazi forces occupied the country. The Nazis closed his university and forced him to work in a quarry. In 1942 he discerned that God was calling him to the priesthood. He was ordained a priest when the war was over. Fr. Wojtyla was made the Archbishop of Krakow in 1964, and three years later he was made a Cardinal.

Like many Poles, Cardinal Wojtyla kept a devotion to the Divine Mercy as Christ revealed to Sr. Faustina. Many Polish people prayed the Divine Mercy chaplet, especially during World War II. But in the early 1960s, all images and prayers associated with Sr. Faustina's visions were banned because of a faulty translation of her writings. A correct translation would have helped clear up the problem, but Poland's Communist government would not send an official translation of her writings to Rome. With the Pope's approval, Cardinal Wojtyla looked into Sr. Faustina's writings. He interviewed people who had met her, and he asked a respected theologian to study her writings. Thanks to Cardinal Wojtyla's work, the Vatican lifted the ban on the Divine Mercy message. Several months later, Cardinal Wojtyla was elected Pope, and he took the name John Paul II.

In 2000, Pope John Paul II canonized Sr. Faustina and established Divine Mercy Sunday as an official feast of the Church on the Sunday after Easter. Pope John Paul II faithfully lived Christ's command to pray for the living and the dead by urging all priests to tell their parishioners about the Divine Mercy, to lead their parishes in prayers in honor of Divine Mercy, and to hear confessions on Divine Mercy Sunday. Pope John Paul II died on the vigil of Divine Mercy Sunday in 2005. He was beatified on Divine Mercy Sunday in 2011 and canonized on Divine Mercy Sunday in 2014.

St. Maximilian Kolbe

1894-1941

Feast Day:
August 14

Raymund Kolbe was born in Poland. He entered a Franciscan monastery when he was 16. There he received the name Maximilian. He was ordained a priest in 1919. Fr. Kolbe taught men who were preparing to be priests, and opened a religious community in Poland. He traveled to Japan and to India and opened communities there too.

When he returned to Poland, the Nazis had invaded the country. The Nazis were rounding up Jews and putting them in death camps. Fr. Kolbe organized a shelter for thousands of Polish people who had nowhere to go. In 1941, the Nazis raided the shelter. They took Fr. Kolbe and his companions to a death camp.

Life in the prison was very hard for Fr. Kolbe, but he always put the other prisoner's needs ahead of his own. Heeding Christ's call to feed the hungry, he would often refuse his tiny portion of food to give to another. The guards beat and tortured him. But Fr. Kolbe wouldn't ask for medical help until all his fellow prisoners had been treated. Though he was suffering, Fr. Kolbe helped the other prisoners. He would ask each one, "I am a Catholic priest. Can I do anything for you?" He heard their confessions. He assured them of God's love.

One day a prisoner escaped. The guards said that 10 prisoners would be starved to death as a punishment. The guards choose 10 men. One of the men cried out in grief for his wife and children. Fr. Kolbe stepped forward and volunteered to take the condemned man's place. Fr. Kolbe was put in a cell with the other nine men. He comforted these afflicted men by praying and reading the Psalms with them. After two weeks of hunger and thirst, Fr. Kolbe was still alive. The Nazis injected poison into Fr. Kolbe's arm and he died.

The man Fr. Kolbe saved survived the war.

St. Martin of Tours

c. 315–395

Feast Day:
November 11

Martin was born at the height of the Roman Empire in modern day Hungry. Neither of his parents approved of Christianity. Still, at the age of 10, Martin became a Christian catechumen (a person preparing for baptism).

Martin longed to become a monk, but he was forced into military service at age 15. He became an officer in Gaul (modern day France). While on guard duty one winter night, he encountered a half-naked beggar freezing in the cold. Martin felt compassion for the man. He took off his own warm cloak and used his sword to slice it in two. He wrapped the beggar in one half and placed the other half on his own shoulders. Later that night, Martin dreamed Jesus was wearing the cloak he had given to the beggar. Jesus said "See! This is the mantle that Martin, yet a catechumen, gave me," vividly reflecting the Corporal Work of Mercy to clothe the naked. Jesus' words in the dream prompted Martin to be baptized.

Martin never stopped wanting to be a monk. As a Christian, be believed he should seek peace rather than conflict. At the end of his military service, Martin refused to go into a battle. Instead he suggested he meet the opposing army without sword or shield and negotiate peace. His superiors threw him in jail until the day of the battle, and then they released him from the army.

Martin was finally able to become the hermit monk he always desired to be. Tales of his holiness and miracles spread until the people of Tours named him their bishop. As bishop, Martin cared for the day-to-day life of his flock and spread the Christian Faith. Martin became a well-respected bishop, consulted in many matters by other bishops and even the emperor. He died well into his 80's and was buried in the Cemetery of the Poor as he requested.

Mary, Mother of Mercy

c.15 B.C.-48 A.D.

Feast Day: Saturday before the fourth Sunday in July

When Adam and Eve sinned and broke the original communion between heaven and earth, God did not abandon mankind. He sent prophets to tell people a savior was coming. Then He created a baby girl, the daughter of Anne and Joachim. From the very beginning of her life, the moment of her conception, God gave this girl the gift of being pure of all sin.

When Mary was a young woman, God sent an angel to her. The angel called Mary "Full of Grace", for no part of her soul was damaged by sin. The angel asked her to be the Mother of Jesus, so that God could come and give His abundant mercy to everyone. Mary submitted herself fully to God's will and became the mother of His Son.

With Jesus growing in her womb, she visited her cousin Elizabeth. Mary told her that God had fulfilled His promise to show His mercy by sending a savior. Mary gave birth to Jesus, nursed Him and bathed Him, played with Him and taught Him. For 30 years, Jesus stayed with her and His foster father Joseph.

Then Jesus began His mission. At Mary's request, Jesus performed His first public miracle for guests at a wedding. When Jesus was dying on the Cross, Mary stayed with him. Jesus entrusted His mother to the care of His apostle John. Mary stayed with John until God took her up to Heaven.

In Heaven, Mary prays constantly to God for everyone who asks for her help, and she asks Him to show His mercy. That is why we pray to her, "Holy Mary, Mother of God, pray for us sinners now and at the hour of our death." God provides us with a Savior in His Son, and He provides us with a Mother, an example, and an intercessor in Mary. Jesus died so that everyone may be a child of God the Father, and Jesus entrusts every person to Mary our Mother.

St. Peter Nolasco

1189-1256

Feast Day:
January 28

Little is known of St. Peter Nolasco's life. He was probably from Languedoc, France and participated in the crusade against the Albigensian heresy, which taught that Jesus was only a spirit and did not have a physical body because the material world was evil.

After the defeat of the heresy, Nolasco was appointed the private tutor of King James I of Aragon and lived in Barcelona, Spain. He became friends with Raymond of Penafort and together they founded the Order of Mercedarians.

At this time in history, Muslim forces known as Moors occupied parts of southern France, Spain, Sicily, and North Africa. Christians who lived near the borders of Muslim territories were in constant danger of raid by the Moor armies. Many were taken prisoner to be ransomed or sold as slaves. Nolasco and Raymond of Penafort took Christ's command to visit the imprisoned to heart. They founded the Mercedarian religious order, under the patronage of the Blessed Mother, for its members to be offered as ransom for Christian captives.

To this day, the members of the order are devoted to offering their lives for the lives of other Christians. Peter himself was offered as ransom on multiple occasions. It is believed that on one trip to Moorish prisons in southern Spain, he won the release of more than four hundred Christians who were held prisoner there.

Peter Nolasco was canonized by Pope Urban VIII in 1628.

Bl. Miguel Pro Juárez

1891-1927

Feast Day:
November 23

Miguel was born in Guadeloupe, Mexico. His family was devoutly Catholic. Young Miguel enjoyed doodling and drawing cartoons, and he was very good at it! When his sister entered a convent, Miguel began to hear the Lord calling him to be a priest. He entered a Jesuit seminary. (A seminary is a school that prepares future priests.) He was there when an anti-Catholic government began taking over Mexico. The seminary was forced to close. He and his classmates escaped to the United States. He continued his preparation, and was made a priest in Europe in 1925.

Back in Mexico, being Catholic was illegal. Churches had been forced to close. Priests had to hide. Even though it was dangerous, Fr. Pro wanted to return to Mexico. He got permission to go, and once there he began helping people in secret. He would wear disguises to stay safe while he tended to people's needs. Sometimes he would dress as a beggar. When he went into rich neighborhoods to ask people to help the poor, he would dress as a businessman. He even dressed as a policeman to offer Holy Communion to prisoners.

Someone told the police what Fr. Pro was doing, and he was arrested. The government lied and said Fr. Pro had tried to kill the president of Mexico. Fr. Pro was sentenced to death for a crime he did not commit. He was sent to a firing squad. He forgave his executioners, and prayed out loud for God to forgive them. He stood before them with his arms stretched out at his sides. He held a rosary in one hand and a crucifix in the other. His last words were "Viva Cristo Rey," which means "Praise Christ the King!"

St. Teresa of Ávila

1515-1582

Feast Day:
October 15

Teresa Sánchez de Cepeda y Ahumada was born in the Ávila region of Spain. When she was younger she was caught up in her social life. She wanted to love God, but felt like she did not deserve to be close to Him. Her father sent her to a convent to help her straighten out her life. But the convent turned out to be more like a hotel, with frequent visitors and socializing. Teresa prayed to be closer to Jesus, but felt like He wasn't answering her. After 18 years, she felt like giving up.

When she was 41, a priest encouraged her to turn back to prayer. But it was hard for her. She felt like her mind was too busy and distracted to be able to focus on Jesus. But soon she felt very close to God. Praying became such an intense experience that she would cry. She would feel pain, and all her senses would be overwhelmed. Sometimes her whole body would even levitate (be raised up from the ground). These experiences scared Teresa and she especially disliked when they happened in public. But she knew Jesus was with her when He came to her in visions. Then she felt peaceful and encouraged.

Two years later she decided to start a new convent focused on prayer and living simply. Her reforms made a lot of people angry, but new Discalced Carmelite communities eventually spread throughout Europe. She wrote books about her life and her visions, even though many people said women shouldn't do those things. In 1970, Pope Paul VI named her a Doctor of the Church. This is a very special title that means her writings are especially useful to Christians.

St. Thérèse of Lisieux

1873-1897

Feast Day:
October 1

Thérèse Martin was born in Alençon, France. Her mother and father had nine children, and Thérèse was one of five who survived. Thérèse's mother died when Thérèse was only 4 years old. Her father moved the family to Lisieux, and Thérèse's older sisters helped take care of her.

For much of her life, Thérèse was delicate and sensitive. She would cry if she thought someone was criticizing her. Then she would feel even worse about herself because she had cried. Two of her sisters were nuns at a Discalced Carmelite convent. Thérèse also received a call to religious life, but she was too young to join the convent. But Thérèse did not give up. When she was 15, she went on a pilgrimage to Rome. Her group was able to visit the Pope, and she asked him for special permission to enter the convent. One of the Pope's officers saw her and was impressed with her courage. She was given permission to enter the convent. Thérèse would be a cloistered nun, meaning that, in answer to Christ's call to pray for the living and the dead, she would spend her days in prayer, away from other people and the world.

Thérèse knew that Jesus wanted the little ones to come to Him. In fact, Jesus Himself had become a child! So Thérèse was glad she was little. She wrote: "In spite of my littleness, I can aim at being a saint. ...I will look for some means of going to heaven by a little way which is very short and very straight, a little way that is quite new." St. Thérèse is known for this "Little Way" of seeking holiness in ordinary, everyday things.

In 1896 she started coughing up blood. She had tuberculosis, which is a painful and deadly illness. She died less than a year later at age 24. The wisdom in her writings was so profound that Pope John Paul II named her a Doctor of the Church. This is a very special title that means her writings are especially useful to Christians.

St. Jean-Marie Vianney

1786-1859

Feast Day:
August 4

Jean lived with his parents and five siblings in a French village. When Jean was very young, France was at war. The government outlawed Catholicism, and priests were forced to hold Mass in secret. Jean and his family traveled for miles to farm houses where priests said Mass in rooms with windows covered to block the candlelight from being seen. Jean admired the priests who risked their lives to offer the Mass and hear Confessions.

When Jean was 16, the French Revolution ended. He began studying for the priesthood, but he was soon drafted into Napoleon's army. As he walked to the army base, he paused to pray. A Catholic saw him and offered to guide him to the base, but instead led Jean to a hidden village where many Catholics lived. Jean started a school for the children in the village. When French soldiers came looking for Jean, he hid inside stacks of old hay. Several months later, he was able to return to seminary. Jean was ordained at age 39 and assigned to the parish of Ars.

Fr. Vianney worked hard in his parish. The revolution had caused many people to feel suspicious or careless about being Catholic. In answer to Jesus' call to counsel the doubtful, Fr. Vianney tried to revive people's interest in the Faith. He preached excellent homilies. He started a home for girls, and he heard the Confession of everyone who came to him. He sat in the confessional for up to 16 hours a day, every day, to listen, advise, and absolve the thousands of people who traveled miles to confess and receive his instruction. He heard Confessions every day until he died at age 73.

St. Vincent de Paul

c. 1580-1660

Feast Day:
September 27

Vincent de Paul was born to poor peasant farmers in France in 1581. Vincent's parents saw that he had a natural talent for academic study, and they sacrificed to be able send him to school. Vincent attended university, was ordained a priest at age 24, and continued his studies.

While on a short sea voyage, Fr. De Paul was captured by pirates and sold as a slave in Africa. There, he was re-sold to different masters many times over the next two years. Eventually, he converted his Muslim master to Christianity and the two of them escaped back to France. Fr. De Paul was given his freedom, but his experiences of the poor and outcast never left him.

Fr. De Paul especially responded to Christ's command to visit the sick. Fr. De Paul founded many hospitals for the poor and worked to treat not only their physical needs, but their spiritual needs as well. He founded communities and organizations to go out to the poor and the sick to care for them. These include the Ladies of Charity and the Daughters of Charity. He founded the religious order of priests called the Congregation of the Mission, or later, the Vincentians.

His fame around France grew, despite his humility regarding his work. He was able to use his notoriety to raise money to keep the hospitals, communities of service, and Works of Mercy serving the poor effectively. Fr. De Paul was also concerned with serving the clergy. He worked to reform the corrupt practices of the clergy in France. He also helped to better prepare men who felt called to enter into the priesthood.

St. Vincent de Paul died near 80 years of age in 1660. He was canonized by Pope Clement XII in 1737 and is the patron saint of all charitable societies.

St. Francis Xavier

1506–1552

Feast Day:
December 3

Francis Xavier was born into a wealthy and noble family in Spain. While at university in Paris, Francis roomed with Ignatius of Loyola. Initially, Francis and Ignatius did not get along, but eventually Ignatius won him over with his simple way of life and preaching of the Gospel. The pair, along with five other men, soon took vows of poverty, chastity, and obedience to the pope. Together they founded a new religious order, the Society of Jesus, or the Jesuits, and lived under a rule of life written by Ignatius. Pope John III requested that the Jesuits be sent out as missionaries around the world.

Francis was sent on the first Jesuit mission, which brought him to Goa in western India. There, he preached to the Portuguese settlers who lived there, many of whom led sinful lives. He cared for the sick, catechized children, and built almost 40 churches. He evangelized a group of nearby natives who had been baptized Christians a decade before but had never really been taught about Jesus or the Faith.

Over the next eight years, Francis pushed eastward, spreading the Gospel to parts of Malaysia. Eventually, Francis became the first Jesuit missionary in Japan. To overcome the language barrier, he used simple paintings of Mary and the child Jesus to preach the Good News. He also used the Rosary, his catechism, and above all the example of his own life to evangelize.

Francis Xavier died of a fever while waiting for a boat to take him to China to continue his missionary work. It is thought by the time of his death, by his response to Jesus' command to teach the ignorant, he had personally converted to Christianity over 50,000 people. He was canonized by Pope Gregory XV in 1622 and is the patron saint of foreign missions.

Teacher Notes

APPENDIX B

Teacher Toolkit: Special Projects for Entering into the Story of Salvation

The following pages include project descriptions and student instruction pages for:

Genesis Movie/Skit Project

Biblical Character Facebook Profile

Journey of an Israelite from Slavery to Freedom Journal

Corporal Works of Mercy Project

Spiritual Works of Mercy Project

Final Project Idea

Genesis Movie/Skit Project

Procedure

1. Divide the class into 4 groups.
2. Assign each group one of the following sections from Genesis:
   - Genesis 1-11 (Creation-Tower of Babel)
   - Genesis 12-22 (Story of Abraham)
   - Genesis 24-35 (Story of Jacob and Esau)
   - Genesis 36-50 (Story of Joseph)
3. Hand out the project directions and go over with the students.
4. You will need to determine how much time you want to give them in class to work on this project versus how much they will need to do at home.
5. Recommended time to give them to complete this if they are mainly working outside of class is 4-6 weeks.

Goal

Students will learn that God uses imperfect people to accomplish great things by examining one of the main stories in Genesis more closely.

They will also learn how to:

- work and collaborate as a group
- study Scripture more closely
- use creative skills to help one part of the story of salvation come alive

Tips

- Assign the groups rather than letting students choose
- Take into account demands on student time and family life when assigning long-term projects to be done at home.

Genesis Movie/Skit Project

Directions

1. Read the chapters assigned to you as a group.
2. Summarize the chapters.
3. Pick out all the important characters in your story and list them. Then write a description of each one next to their names. Each description should be 1-4 sentences long, depending on the significance of the character.
4. Create a script for your story.
5. Prepare a skit or movie to present in front of the class.
6. At the project conclusion, each person will write an individual reflection paper.

Guidelines

1. All work must be typed, double-spaced, in Times New Roman, 12 point font.
2. Summaries should be 3-5 pages long.
3. Character sketches should be 1-3 pages long.
4. Scripts must include the main points of the story.
5. Skits/Movies must be thoughtful, accurate and creative. You must use costumes, props, and move around. (Standing in one place does not constitute a skit!) You may also use music or anything else to make your skit as entertaining as possible. It should hold the classes' attention while remaining true to the story. Have fun with this. Feel free to tell the story using a creative theme.
6. Reflection papers must be 2-4 pages long. Pick out three lessons you think God is teaching the people in your story, give support for those lessons, and then explain how you can apply these lessons in your own life. Finally, you need to show how you see the concept of covenant being played out in your story.
7. All work needs to be turned in in a folder. In the right pocket please place, in this order: character sketch, summary, and script. In the left pocket please place your reflection papers.
8. Written portion in the folder will be due ______________________________.
9. Movie or skit will be due on ______________________________.

Grading and Points

This project will be worth ______________________ pts.

Written Work: summary, character sketch, script, and cover page: ______________ pts.

Skit/Movie: ______________ pts.

Reflection Paper: ______________ pts.

Organization and Effort: ______________ pts.

Biblical Character Facebook Profile

Procedure

1. Create a list of characters from which students may select.
2. Distribute the student instruction page.
3. Upload the PowerPoint template (found on the Sophia Institute for Teachers Catholic Curriculum Exchange), to Edmodo, a wiki page, or email it to your students.
4. Give students a due date.

Sample character list:

Adam	Lot
Eve	Hagar
Cain	Ishmael
Abel	Isaac
Seth	Rebekah
Lamech	Jacob
Noah	Rachel
Shem	Esau
Ham	Joseph
Abraham	Moses
Sarah	Aaron

Goal

Students will experience and present a thorough exploration of an individual from Salvation History and the importance of his/her story.

Note

This is not an exhaustive list; you can do this particular project at any point in Salvation History.

STUDENT INSTRUCTIONS

Biblical Facebook Profile

For this project, your assigned group will create an imaginary Facebook profile for a biblical character of your choice from the list provided. This will serve as a thorough exploration of this individual and the importance of his/her story.

- **Instructions for each PowerPoint slide are at the bottom of each slide. You must follow these instructions in order to receive full points for each section.**
- Certain parts of this PowerPoint presentation are hyperlinked. This means that during a slide show presentation, you can click on certain parts and it will automatically take you to another slide. **DO NOT change any of the formatting on any slide unless directed to do so.**

Journey of an Israelite from Slavery to Freedom Journal

Procedure

1. Hand out student instruction sheet.
2. Go over instructions with them.
3. Suggest to your students that if they wish to create an authentic look, they can dye their journals with tea and then burn the edges to make them look old! Important: They should only do this step *after* completing the writing assignment.

Goal

Students will understand and appreciate the story of the Israelites during the covenant with Moses and identify this ancient journey with their own spiritual journey.

STUDENT INSTRUCTIONS

Creative Journal: The Journey of an Israelite

You will be responsible for creating a journal of an Israelite journeying from slavery to the desert to freedom. You will have to write 12 half-page entries for a total of a 6-page journal.

1. Make up a name for yourself.
2. Decide if you are a child or an adult.
3. In your first entry, make sure you introduce yourself, tell of your struggles as a slave under the Egyptians, explain how Moses has arrived, and how you see the plagues affecting the people.
4. Your second entry should discuss your experience of the Passover and your journey to freedom through the Red Sea.
5. Entries 3-11 should deal with different experiences and events during your time in the desert.
    - 4 of these entries should be based on events from the book of Exodus.
    - 2 entries should be based on events in the book of Numbers leading up to the event with the wicked spies and the punishment.
    - 3 entries should be based on events in the book of Numbers after the punishment.
6. Entry 12 should vary based on whether you have decided to be an adult or child. If you are an adult, discuss the time after the punishment and describe how you are on your deathbed. If you began as a child, this entry should be focused on how the 40 years are up and you are about to enter the Promised Land.

All entries should be typed or written very neatly in an artistic fashion. You will be graded on creativity and on how well you present actual events. (Although you will incorporate fictional elements for dramatization, these entries are based entirely on real events.) This assignment requires you to read through the books of Exodus and Numbers and pick out major events to focus on. Some Events that should be included besides those specifically mentioned above, but not limited to: golden calf, quail and manna, water from the rock, bronze serpent, the bad spies, and being sentenced for 40 years.

Corporal Works of Mercy Project

Goal

Students will survey the corporal Works of Mercy by analyzing individuals from Scripture, characters from mythology, literature, and film, as well as their own friends and family, before beginning a plan to perform these works themselves.

Procedure

1. Hand out student instruction sheet.
2. Go over instructions with them.
3. Offer a few examples to prime students' thinking for the first two columns, such as:
   - God clothes Adam and Eve after He banishes them from the Garden. (Clothe the naked – Scripture)
   - Antigone buries her brother. (Bury the dead – mythology)
   - In the movie *Groundhog Day*, as Bill Murray's character grows in virtue he begins practicing Corporal Works of Mercy including feeding the hungry and giving drink to the thirsty. (Feed the hungry and give drink to the thirsty – film)
   - You could also prime students' thinking by brainstorming evil characters who fail to practice these works.
4. For their reflection paper, students should choose one person they know and write a reflection paper on how this person has inspired them to focus on practicing at least one particular Corporal Work of Mercy.
5. If students have trouble identifying a person they know personally, they may choose a person from American or world history who especially practiced Works of Mercy, and do research on him/her. For example, Servant of God Dorothy Day, Mother Teresa, Miguel Pro, and others.

STUDENT INSTRUCTIONS

Works of Mercy Project

By completing this chart, you will explore all of the Corporal Works of Mercy from the perspective of Scripture, literature/film, and your own friends and family. Let each example in the first three columns inspire you with ways to fill in the last column! Finally, choose one person you know and write a reflection paper on how this person has inspired you to focus on practicing at least one particular Corporal Work of Mercy.

Work of Mercy	Someone in the Bible who performed this Work of Mercy	Character from literature, mythology, or film who performs this Work of Mercy	Someone I know who performs this Work of Mercy	How I can perform this Work of Mercy
Feed the hungry				
Give drink to the thirsty				
Clothe the naked				

Work of Mercy	Someone in the Bible who performed this Work of Mercy	Character from literature, mythology, or film who performs this Work of Mercy	Someone I know who performs this Work of Mercy	How I can perform this Work of Mercy
Shelter the homeless				
Visit the sick				
Visit the imprisoned				
Bury the dead				

Spiritual Works of Mercy Project

Procedure

1. Distribute the student instruction sheet.
2. Go over the assignment, making some suggestions if needed. Students may wish to:
    - Investigate the opportunities to serve in various ministries in their parish.
    - Encourage a friend who has not been going to Mass to go with them.
    - Stand up to bullies; protect the weak; speak out against evil.
    - Give of themselves to someone who has lost a loved one.
    - Forgive someone who has hurt them.
    - Remember loved ones, living and dead, in their prayers.

Goal

Students will learn more about exercising their share in the common priesthood of Jesus Christ through Baptism by practicing the Spiritual Works of Mercy. Have students keep a journal for at least three months, chronicling their practice of these works and answering these questions.

- Which have to do with being a *priest* by sanctifying the world?
- Which works have to do with being a *prophet* by preaching or teaching?
- Which have to do with being a *king* by guiding people to Jesus?
- Which is the hardest of these to do?
- Which can you do today?
- Which can you do every day?

Spiritual Works of Mercy Project

Directions

Through your Baptism, you are a part of the common priesthood of Jesus Christ. This means you share in His mission as priest, prophet, and king.

For the next ____________ months, you will keep a journal explaining how you have practiced the Spiritual Works of Mercy.

On the first page of your journal, write out the Spiritual Works of Mercy below.

The Spiritual Works of Mercy

- Admonish the sinner
- Instruct the ignorant
- Counsel the doubtful
- Comfort the sorrowful
- Bear wrongs patiently
- Forgive all injuries
- Pray for the living and the dead

As you think and write about your practice of these works, consider:

- Which have to do with being a *priest* by sanctifying the world?
- Which works have to do with being a *prophet* by preaching or teaching?
- Which have to do with being a *king* by guiding people to Jesus?
- Which is the hardest of these to do?
- Which can you do today?
- Which can you do every day?

Final Project Idea

Procedure

1. This project gives the student a variety of choices and ways to be assessed.
2. Hand out the student instructions.
3. Go over the different ideas with them.
4. Encourage them to choose a project that plays to their strengths.

Goal

To get students to explore a book of the Bible or events in Salvation History while at the same time giving them ownership and creativity in the designing of their project.

Tips

- Give students two due dates, one that requires them to declare and commit to a particular project (usually 2-3 days after you assign) and one that is the due date for the actual project
- Give them class time to ask plenty of questions about their project choice.
- Encourage them to be as creative as possible with these.

Final Project

1. You may choose to work by yourself or with a group.
2. You may chose to do any of the projects listed below or come up with one on your own as long as it is pre-approved by me.
3. Your project must be based on one of the following books of the Old Testament: Tobit, Judith, Esther, 1 and 2 Maccabees, 2 Kings, Ezra, Nehemiah, Daniel, Job, Jonah, or any of the other Prophets.
4. All projects must be done artistically or typed. This means projects should be done well and neatly, which means that if you do not have the ability to draw or paint then you should not do a project that requires these skills. Choose something that will draw out your strengths.
5. This project will be due ________________.
6. This project will be worth ________________ points.
7. All projects need to be turned in neatly and organized with your name and the date on all pieces.
8. You may chose from one of the following options:
   - **A skit or movie over a book (or books, depending on length).** *Skits and Movies need to be at least 10-15 minutes in length, include costumes, props, and be well edited and rehearsed. You must also turn in a TYPED script of your movie. No less than 4 people and no more than 6 people.*
   - **A children's book with illustrations re-telling a particular book.** *These need to include 10-15 illustrated pages with a minimum of 3 sentences and a maximum of half a page of writing per illustration.*
   - **A comic book re-telling a particular book.** *These need to be 10-15 pages long with 4 panels per page and drawings in each panel.*
   - **A trivia board game over a particular book(s).** *All board games must include an original designed board, typed instructions, game pieces, and questions typed out on cards. If working alone you need 60 trivia questions; if working with a partner you need 120 trivia questions. Questions need to be your own and based on the story. All question cards must also include answers!*

- **A book of poems about the books.** *You need to create 15-20 original poems based on one or several of the books listed above.*
- **An artistic painting, sculpture, or 3-D model of one of the events, or people in those books.** *This needs to be accompanied by a 1-2 page TYPED description of your art work. This needs to be detailed. I should be able to see the story come alive in your painting or sculpture.*
- **Prepare a presentation about all the different Jewish holidays. Share with the class how they originated as can be found in the books of the Bible and then prepare foods used to celebrate some of those holidays with the class.** *Your presentation should be 10-15 minutes long detailing the scriptural story of how the holidays and feasts originated and what foods you chose and what they symbolized for the Jews. If working by yourself, prepare 2-3 items; if working with a partner prepare 3-4 items. Your presentation should be 15-20 minutes long. Your presentation should be done using Powerpoint or Prezi.*
- **A newscast or newspaper "covering" one of the books.** *Minimum 2 people, maximum 4. Newspaper should consist of 6 articles per person: 4 must be serious and 2 can be for fun. A newscast can be filmed as a movie or done live in class. It needs to be done with props and turned in with a script. It should be 10-15 minutes long.*
- **Worksheet and puzzle sheets with answer keys over one or several of the books.** *Create 10-15 puzzles sheets with answer keys. 7-10 of them need to be short answer, matching, fill in the blank, and multiple choice. 3-5 of them need to be puzzle type sheets: decode the message, crossword puzzles, word searches, etc. Your worksheets should be decorated with pictures and clip art etc. These should be turned in neatly in a folder.*

APPENDIX C

High School Lesson Connections to USCCB Framework

Lesson 1: Understanding Mercy and Covenants

The Revelation of Jesus Christ in Scripture: I. A. 1-3

Who Is Jesus Christ? I. A. 1. b

Life in Jesus Christ: III. A; III. B. 1. a-b

Lesson 2: God's Mercy Revealed in the Covenant with Adam

The Revelation of Jesus Christ in Scripture: I. A. 1-3

Who Is Jesus Christ? I. A. 1. b

Lesson 3: God's Mercy in the Covenant with Noah

The Revelation of Jesus Christ in Scripture: I. A. 1-3

Who Is Jesus Christ? I. A. 1. b

Lesson 4: The Plan of Mercy Inaugurated: The Covenant with Abraham

The Revelation of Jesus Christ in Scripture: I. A. 1-3

Who Is Jesus Christ? I. A. 1. b

Lesson 5: God's Mercy Tested: The Covenant with Moses

The Revelation of Jesus Christ in Scripture: I. A. 1-3

Who Is Jesus Christ? I. A. 1. b

Lesson 6: God's Mercy Persists: The Covenant with David

The Revelation of Jesus Christ in Scripture: I. A. 1-3

Who Is Jesus Christ? I. A. 1. b

Lesson 7: God's Plan for Mercy Comes to Fulfillment: The New Covenant in Christ

The Revelation of Jesus Christ in Scripture: I. A. 1-3

Who Is Jesus Christ? I. A. 1. b; II. A. 1-3

Lesson 8: Exploring the Corporal and Spiritual Works of Mercy with Sacred Art

Who Is Jesus Christ? 1. B. 1. a-d; II. A. 1-3

Life in Jesus Christ: III. A; III. B. 1. a-b

Living as a Disciple of Jesus Christ in Society: II. A. 3

Lesson 9: Introduction to the Corporal and Spiritual Works of Mercy

Who Is Jesus Christ? 1. B. 1. a-d; II. A. 1-3

Living as a Disciple of Jesus Christ in Society: II. A. 3

Lesson 10: Jesus Teaches us How to Live the Works of Mercy

Who Is Jesus Christ? 1. B. 1. a-d; II. A. 1-3; III. A. 3. a-b; IV. A. 3. a-e

Life in Jesus Christ: III. A; III. B. 1. a-b

Living as a Disciple of Jesus Christ in Society: II. A. 3

Lesson 11: Mercy's Work of Showing God's Love

Who Is Jesus Christ? 1. B. 1. a-d; II. A. 1-3; III. A. 3. a-b; IV. A. 3. a-e

Life in Jesus Christ: III. A; III. B. 1. a-b

Living as a Disciple of Jesus Christ in Society: II. A. 3

Lesson 12: Saints of Mercy

The Revelation of Jesus Christ in Scripture: I. A. 1-3

Who Is Jesus Christ? 1. B. 1. a-d; II. A. 1-3; C. 5. 1-2

Life in Jesus Christ: III. A; III. B. 1. a-b

Living as a Disciple of Jesus Christ in Society: II. A. 3